A Ghost
in the
Throat

A Ghost in the Throat

DOIREANN NÍ GHRÍOFA

TRAMPPRESS

First published in 2020 by Tramp Press
www.tramppress.com

Caoineadh Airt Uí Laoghaire, edited by Seán
Ó Tuama, An Clóchmhar, 1961, reproduced
with permission from Cló Iar-Chonnacht.

A CIP record for this title is available
from the British library.

3 5 7 10 8 6 4 2

ISBN
Paperback: 978-1-9164342-6-4
Ebook: 978-1-9164342-9-5

Tramp Press gratefully acknowledges the
financial assistance of the Arts Council.

Thank you for supporting independent publishing.

Set in 12 pt on 16 pt Quixote by Marsha Swan.
Printed by L&C Group, Poland.

To the three Eileens who lit the lantern I see by:
Eileen Blake, Eileen Forkan,
and Eibhlín Dubh Ní Chonaill.

contents

We are an echo that runs, skittering,
through a train of rooms.

—Czesław Miłosz

Dá dtéadh mo ghlao chun cinn
Go Doire Fhíonáin mór laistiar

Should my howl reach as far
as grand Derrynane

—Eibhlín Dubh Ní Chonaill

A Ghost
in the
Throat

1. a female text

thug mo shúil aire duit,
thug mo chroí taitneamh duit,

how my eye took a shine to you,
how my heart took delight in you,

—Eibhlín Dubh Ní Chonaill

THIS IS A FEMALE TEXT.

This is a female text, composed while folding someone else's clothes. My mind holds it close, and it grows, tender and slow, while my hands perform innumerable chores.

This is a female text borne of guilt and desire, stitched to a soundtrack of cartoon nursery rhymes.

This is a female text and it is a tiny miracle that it even exists, as it does in this moment, lifted to another consciousness by the ordinary wonder of type. Ordinary, too, the ricochet of thought that swoops, now, from my body to yours.

This is a female text, written in the twenty-first century. How late it is. How much has changed. How little.

This is a female text, which is also a *caoineadh:* a dirge and a drudge-song, an anthem of praise, a chant and a keen, a lament and an echo, a chorus and a hymn. Join in.

2012

Every morning of mine is much the same. I kiss my husband, feeling a pang as I do so – no matter how often our morning goodbye is repeated, I always miss him when he leaves. Even as his motorbike roars into the distance, I am already hurrying into my own day. First, I feed our sons, then fill the dishwasher, pick up toys, clean spills, glance at the clock, bring our eldest to school, return home with the toddler and the baby, sigh and snap, laugh and kiss, slump on the sofa to breastfeed the youngest, glance at the clock again, read *The Very Hungry Caterpillar* several times, try to rinse baby-spew from my ponytail into the bathroom sink, fail, make a tower of blocks to be knocked, attempt to mop, give up when the baby cries, kiss the knees of the toddler who slips on the half-washed floor, glance at the clock yet again, wipe more spilled juice, set the toddler at the table with a jigsaw puzzle, and carry the youngest upstairs for his nap.

The baby sleeps in a third-hand cot held together with black gaff tape, and the walls of our rented bedroom are decorated not with pastel murals, but with a constellation of black mould. I can never think of a lullaby, so I resort to tunes from teenage mixtapes instead. I used to rewind 'Karma Police' so obsessively that I wondered whether the brown spool might snap, but every time I pressed play the machine gave me the song again. Now, in my exhaustion, I return to that melody, humming it gently as the baby glugs from my breast. Once his jaw relaxes and his eyes roll back, I creep away, struck again by how often moments of my day are lived by countless other women in countless other rooms, through the shared text of our days. I wonder whether they love their drudge-work as I do, whether they take the same joy in slowly erasing a list like mine, filled with such simplicities as:

School-run
Mop
Hoover Upstairs
Pump
Bins
Dishwasher
Laundry
Clean Toilets
Milk/Spinach/Chicken/Porridge
School-run
Bank + Playground
Dinner
Baths
Bedtime

I keep my list as close as my phone, and draw a deep sense of satisfaction each time I strike a task from it. In such erasure lies joy. No matter how much I give of myself to household chores, each of the rooms under my control swiftly unravels itself again in my aftermath, as though a shadow hand were already beginning the unwritten lists of my tomorrows: more tidying, more hoovering, more dusting, more wiping and mopping and polishing. When my husband is home, we divide the chores, but when I'm alone, I work alone. I don't tell him, but I prefer it that way. I like to be in control. Despite all the chores on my list, and despite my devotion to their completion, the house looks as cheerily dishevelled as any other home of young children, no cleaner, no dirtier.

So far this morning, I have only crossed off school-run, a task that encompassed waking the children, dressing, washing, and feeding them, clearing the breakfast table, finding coats and hats and shoes, brushing teeth, shouting the word 'shoes' several times, filling a lunchbox, checking a schoolbag, shouting for shoes again, and then, finally, walking to the school and back. Since returning home, I have still only half-filled the dishwasher, half-helped my son with his jigsaw, and half-mopped the floor – nothing worthy of deletion from my list. I cling to my list because it is this list that holds my hand through my days, breaking the hours into a series of small, achievable tasks. By the end of a good list, when I am held again in my sleeping husband's arms, this text has become a sequence of scribbles, an obliteration I observe in joy and satisfaction, because the gradual erasure of this handwritten document makes me feel as though I have achieved something of worth in my hours. The list is both my map and my compass.

Now I can feel myself starting to fall behind, so I skim the text of today's tasks to find my bearings, then set the dishwasher humming and draw a line through that word. I smile as I help the toddler find his missing jigsaw piece, clap when he completes it, and finally resort to the remote control. I don't cuddle him close as he watches *The Octonauts*. I don't sit on the sofa with him and close my weary eyes for ten minutes. Instead, I hurry to the kitchen, finish mopping, empty the bins, and then check those tasks off my list with a flourish.

At the sink I scrub my hands, nails, and wrists, then scrub them again. I lift sections of funnels and filters from the steam steriliser to assemble my breast-pump. These machines are not cheap and I no longer have a paying job, so I bought mine second-hand. On my screen, the ad seemed almost as poignant as the baby shoes story usually attributed to Ernest Hemingway –

> Bought for €209, will sell for €45 ONO.
> Used once.

Every morning for months this machine and I have followed the same small ritual in order to gather milk for the babies of strangers. I unclip my bra and scoop my breast into the funnel. It's always the right breast, because my left breast is a lazy bastard: by a month post-partum it has all but given up, so both baby and machine must be fully served by the right. I press the switch, wince as it jerks my nipple awkwardly, adjust myself, and then twist the dial that controls the intensity with which the machine pulls the flesh. At first, the mechanism draws fast and firm, mimicking the baby's pattern of quick suck, until it believes that the milk must have begun to emerge. After a moment or two the pump settles into a steady cadence: long tug, release, repeat. The sensation at nipple level is like a series of small shocks of static electricity, or some strange complication of pins and needles. Unlike feeding the baby, this process always stings, it is never pleasant, and yet the discomfort is endurable. Eventually, the milk stirs to the machine's demands, un-gripping itself somewhere under my armpit. A drop falls from the nipple to be quickly sucked into the machine, then another, and another, until a little meniscus collects in the base of the bottle. I turn my gaze away.

There are mornings, on finding myself particularly tired, that I might daydream a while, or make a ten-minute dent in a library book, but today, as on so many other days, I pick up my scruffy photocopy of *Caoineadh Airt Uí Laoghaire*, inviting the voice of another woman to haunt my throat a while. This is how I fill the only small silence in my day, by turning up the volume of her voice and combining it with the wheeze-whirr of my pump, until I hear nothing beyond it. In the margin, my pencil enters a dialogue with many previous versions of myself, a changeable record of thought in which each question mark asks about the life of the poet who composed the *Caoineadh*, but never questions my own. Minutes later, I startle back to find the pump brimming with pale, warm liquid.

—

When we first met, I was a child, and she had been dead for centuries.

Look: I am eleven, a girl who is terrible at sums and at sports, a girl given to staring out windows, a girl whose only real gift lies in daydreaming. The teacher snaps my name, startling me back to the flimsy prefab. Her voice makes it a fine day in 1773, and sets English soldiers crouching in ambush. I add ditch-water to drench their knees. Their muskets point towards a young man who is tumbling from his saddle now, in slow, slow motion. A woman rides in to kneel over him, her voice rising in an antique formula of breath and syllable the teacher calls a 'caoineadh', a keen to lament the dead. Her voice generates an echo strong enough to reach a girl in the distance with dark hair and bitten nails. Me.

In the classroom, we are presented with an image of this woman standing alone, a convenient breeze setting her as a windswept, rosy-cheeked colleen. This, we are told, is Eibhlín Dubh Ní Chonaill, among the last noblewomen of the old Irish order. Her story seems sad, yes, but also a little dull. Schoolwork. Boring. My gaze has already soared away with the crows, while my mind loops back to my most-hated pop-song, 'and you give yourself away ...' No matter how I try to oust them, those lyrics won't let me be.

—

By the time I find her again, I only half-remember our first meeting. As a teenager I develop a school-girl crush on this *caoineadh*, swooning over the tragic romance embedded in its lines. When Eibhlín Dubh describes falling in love at first sight and abandoning her family to marry a stranger, I love her for it, just as every teenage girl loves the story of running away forever. When she finds her murdered lover and drinks handfuls of his blood, I scribble pierced hearts in the margin. Although I don't understand it yet, something ricochets in me whenever I return to this image of a woman kneeling to drink from the body of a lover, something that reminds me of the inner glint I feel whenever a boyfriend presses his teenage hips to mine and his lips to my throat.

My homework is returned to me with a large red X, and worse, the teacher's scrawl cautions: 'Don't let your imagination run away with you!' I have felt these verses so deeply that I know my answer must be correct, and so, in righteous exasperation, I thump page after page down hard as I make my way back to the poem, scowling. In response to the request 'Describe the poet's first encounter with Art Ó Laoghaire,' I had written: 'She jumps on his horse and rides away with him forever,' but on returning, I am baffled to find that the teacher is correct: this image does not exist in the text. If not from the poem, then where did it come from? I can visualise it so clearly: Eibhlín Dubh's arms circling her lover's waist, her fingers woven over his warm belly, the drumming of hooves, and the long ribbon of hair streaming behind her. It may not be real to my teacher, but it is to me.

———

If my childhood understanding of this poem was, well, childish, and my teenage interpretation little more than a swoon, my readings swerved again in adulthood.

I had no classes to attend anymore, no textbooks or poems to study, but I had set myself a new curriculum to master. In attempting to raise our family on a single income, I was teaching myself to live by the rigours of frugality. I examined classified ads and supermarket deals with care. I met internet strangers and handed them coins in exchange for bundles of their babies' clothes. I sold bundles of our own. I roamed car boot sales, haggling over toddler toys and stair-gates. I only bought car seats on sale. There was a doggedness to be learned from such thrift, and I soon took to it.

My earliest years of motherhood, in all their fatigue and awe and fretfulness, took place in various rented rooms of the inner city. Although I had been raised in the countryside, I found that I adored it there: the terraces of smiling neighbours with all their tabbies and terriers, all our bins lined up side by side, the overheard cries of rage or lust in the dark, and the weekend parties with their happy, drunken choruses. Our taps always dripped, there were rats in the tiny yard, and the night city's glimmering made stars invisible, but when I woke to feed my first son, and then my second, I could split the curtains and see the moon between the spires. In those city rooms, I wrote a poem. I wrote another. I wrote a book. If the poems that came to me on those nights might be considered love poems, then they were in love with rain and alpine flowers, with the strange vocabularies of a pregnant body, with clouds and with grandmothers. No poem arrived in praise of the man who slept next to me as I wrote, the man whose moonlit skin always drew my lips towards him. The love I held for him felt too vast to pour into the neat vessel of a poem. I couldn't put it into words. I still can't. As he dreamt, I watched poems hurrying towards me through the dark. The city had lit something in me, something that pulsed, vulnerable as a fontanelle, something that trembled, as I did, between bliss and exhaustion.

We had already moved house twice in three years, and still the headlines reported that rents were increasing. Our landlords always saw opportunity in such bulletins, and who could blame them? Me. I blamed them every time we were evicted with a shrug. No matter how glowing their letters of reference, I always resented being forced to leave another home. Now we were on the cusp of moving again. I'd searched for weeks, until eventually I found a nearby town with lower rents. We signed another lease, packed our car, and left the city. I didn't want to go. I drove slow, my elbow straining to change gear, wedged between our old TV and a bin-bag of teddies, my voice leading a chorus through 'five little ducks went swimming one day'. I found my way along unfamiliar roads, 'over the hills and far away', scanning signs for Bishopstown and Bandon, for Macroom and Blarney, while singing 'Mammy Duck said Quack, Quack, Quack ...' until my eye tripped over a sign for Kilcrea.

Kilcrea – Kilcrea – the word repeated in my mind as I unlocked a new door, it repeated and repeated as I scoured dirt from the tiles, and grimaced at the biography of old blood and semen stains on the mattresses. *Kilcrea, Kilcrea,* the word vexed me for days, as I unpacked books and coats and baby monitors, spoons and towels and tangled phone chargers, until finally, I remembered – *Yes!* – in that old poem from school, wasn't Kilcrea the name of the graveyard where the poet buried her lover? I cringed, remembering my crush on that poem, as I cringed when I recalled all the skinny rock-stars torn and tacked onto my teenage walls, the vocabulary they allowed me to express the beginnings of desire. I flinched, in general, at my teenage self. She made me uncomfortable, that girl, how she displayed her wants so brashly, that girl who flaunted a schoolbag Tipp-Exed with longing, who scribbled her own marker over layers of laneway graffiti, who stared obscenely at strangers from bus windows, who met their eyes and held them until she saw her own lust stir there. The girl caught in forbidden behaviours behind the school and threatened with expulsion. The girl called a *slut* and a *whore* and a *frigid bitch*. The girl condemned to 'silent treatment'. The girl punished and punished and punished again. The girl who didn't care. I was here, singing to a child while scrubbing old shit from a stranger's toilet. Where was she?

—

In the school car park, I found myself a little early to pick up my eldest and sought shelter from the rain under a tree. My son was still dreaming under his plastic buggy-cover, and I couldn't help but admire his ruby cheeks and the plump, dimpled arms I tucked back under his blanket. *There*. In the scrubby grass that bordered the concrete, bumblebees were browsing – if I had a garden of my own, I thought, I'd fill it with low forests of clover and all the ugly weeds they adore, I'd throw myself to my knees in service to bees. I looked past them towards the hills in the distance, and, thinking of that road-sign again, I rummaged for my phone. There were many more verses to the *Caoineadh* than I recalled, thirty, or more. The poem's landscape came to life as I read, it was alive all around me, alive and fizzing with rain, and I felt myself alive in it. Under that drenched tree, I found her sons, 'Conchubhar beag an cheana is Fear Ó Laoghaire, an leanbh' – which I translated to myself as 'our dotey little Conchubhar / and Fear Ó Laoghaire, the babba'. I was startled to find Eibhlín Dubh pregnant again with her third child, just as I was. I had never imagined her as a mother in any of my previous readings, or perhaps I had simply ignored that part of her identity, since the collision of mother and desire wouldn't have fitted with how my teenage self wanted to see her. As my fingertip-scar navigated the text now, however, I could almost imagine her lullaby-hum in the dark. I scrolled the text from beginning to end, then swiped back to read it all again. Slower, this time.

The poem began within Eibhlín Dubh's gaze as she watched a man stroll across a market. His name was Art and, as he walked, she wanted him. Once they eloped, they led a life that could only be described as opulent: oh, the lavish bedchambers, oh, the delectable meals, oh, the couture, oh, the long, long mornings of sleep in sumptuous duck-down. As Art's wife, she wanted for nothing. I envied her her home and wondered how many servants it took to keep it all going, how many shadow-women doing their shadow-work, the kind of shadow-women I come from. Eibhlín dedicates entire verses to her lover in descriptions so vivid that they shudder with a deep love and a desire that still feels electric, but the fact that this poem was composed after his murder means that grief casts its murk-shadow over every line of praise. How powerful such a cataloguing must have felt in the aftermath of his murder, when each spoken detail conjured him back again, alive and impeccably dressed, with a shining pin glistening in his hat, and 'the suit of fine couture / stitched and spun abroad for you'. She shows us Art as desired, not only by herself, but by others, too, by posh city women who –

> always
> stooped their curtsies low for you.
> How well, they could see
> what a hearty bed-mate you'd be,
> what a man to share a saddle with,
> what a man to spark a child with.

Although the couple were living through the regime of fear and cruelty inflicted by the Penal Laws, her husband was defiant. Despite his many enemies, Art seemed somehow unassailable to Eibhlín, until the day that 'she came to me, your steed, / with her reins trailing the cobbles, / and your heart's blood smeared from cheek to saddle'. In this terrifying moment, Eibhlín neither hesitated nor sought help. Instead, she leapt into that drenched saddle and let her husband's horse carry her to his body. In anguish and in grief, then, she fell upon him, keening and drinking mouthfuls of his blood. Even in such a moment of raw horror, desire remained – she roared over his corpse, ordering him to rise from the dead so she might 'have a bed dressed / in bright blankets / and embellished quilts / to spark your sweat and set it spilling'. But Art was dead, and the text she composed became an evolving record of praise, sorrow, lust, and reminiscence.

Through the darkness of grief, this rage is a lucifer match, struck and sparking. She curses the man who ordered Art's murder: 'Morris, you runt; on you, I wish anguish! – / May bad blood spurt from your heart and your liver! / Your eyes grow glaucoma! / Your knee-bones both shatter!' Such furies burn and dissipate and burn again, for this is a poem fuelled by the twin fires of anger and desire. Eibhlín rails against all involved in Art's betrayal, including her own brother-in-law, 'that shit-talking clown'. Rage. Rage and anguish. Rage and anguish and love. She despairs for her two young sons, 'and the third, still within me, / I fear will never breathe'. What losses this woman has suffered. What losses are yet to come. She is in pain, as is the poem itself; this text is a text in pain. It aches. When the school-bell rang, my son found me in the rain, my face turned towards the hills where Eibhlín Dubh once lived.

That night, the baby squirmed inside me until I abandoned sleep, scrambling for my phone instead. My husband instinctively curled his sleeping body into mine; despite his snores, I felt him grow hard against the dip of my back. I frowned, holding very still until I was sure he was asleep, then inching away to whisper the poem to myself, conjuring a voice through hundreds of years, from her pregnant body to mine. As everyone else dreamed, my eyes were open in the dark.

—

When I finally fell asleep, another mother was waking. Sensing a mouth gripped to her milk, she lifted herself by claw and by clench, stretched, and then opened her wings, sleek as an opera cloak. An infant clung to her fur as she twitched, readying herself for flight from arrangements of stone which were dreamt, drawn, and built by human hands long before. Soon, she was in motion, plunging and soaring, swooping and falling, devouring every aquatic midge she found over The Lough, while her infant gripped tight, still and suckling, eyes closed to her mother's momentum. To glimpse a bat in flight is to sense a flicker at the periphery of one's vision, phantom inverted commas tilting through the dark. A complex system of echolocation allows her to navigate the night, guided by the echoes that answer her voice.

—

Months passed the way months will, in a spin of grocery lists, vomiting bugs, Easter eggs, hoovering, and electricity bills. I grew and grew, until one morphine-bright day in July my third son made his slow way from my belly to my chest, and I found myself in the whip exhaustion of night-feeds again. Throughout those yellow-nappy weeks, when everything spun wildly in the erratic orbit of others' needs, only the lines of the *Caoineadh* remained steadfast.

In falling into the whirligig of those days, I had stolen from myself something so precious and so nebulous that I wasn't myself without it. Desire. After the birth, every flicker of want was erased from me with such a neat completeness that I felt utterly vacant. To fulfil all its needs for intimacy, my body served and was served by the small body of another. I still experienced powerful physical urges, but they were never sexual. I was ruled by milk now, an ocean that surged and ripped to the laws of its own tides.

Sex was a problem. It hurt and hurt. For months after the birth, it felt as though some inner door had slammed shut. All I sought from life was to drag myself and my animal exhaustion through the daylight hours until darkness eventually led me to bed and into another night of fractured sleep. How quickly desire had abandoned me, its evaporation a swift invisibility, as a puddle gives itself back to sky. I was not myself. I was a large, tattered jumper, my seams all fretted and frayed, and yet this garment was so comfortable, so soft and so easy, that I wanted nothing more than to immerse myself in its gentle bulk forever. I was bone-weary, yes, but I was also mostly content. However, I found such abstinence too much of a horror to inflict on the man I loved so much. Whereas my husband insisted that all was well, and that he would happily wait until the exhaustion had passed and I wanted him again, I found that I could not accept this gentle gift. So I lied. I made of desire another chore to suffer, an unwritten item that hovered invisibly at the foot of my lists. Whenever I forced myself through the motions, I was choosing both a literal forcing, because it hurt so much for me to shove that locked door open, and an emotional forcing, because he is a good man, and I was intentionally deceiving him. As for the sex, it hurt and hurt until the pain made me bite the sad skin between my thumb and finger. Days after those teeth marks faded, a pattern of bruises still punctuated the skin. I convinced myself that it must be good to endure such pain if it facilitated the pleasure of another. Only now do I see that I was making his body another item on my list of responsibilities, and that I was doing so without his consent. I was so ashamed of my failings – both of honesty and of the body – that I tried to hide this calamity. I said goodnight early instead. I made excuses. I slept at the edge of the bed. There, I kept the *Caoineadh* under my pillow, and whenever I stirred to feed the baby, Eibhlín Dubh's words broke through my trippy, exhausted haze. Her life and her desires were so distant from mine, and yet she felt so close. Before long, the poem began to leak into my days. My curiosity grew until it sent me out of the house and towards the only rooms that could help.

—

Look: it is a Tuesday morning, and a security guard in a creased blue uniform is unlocking a door and standing aside with a light-hearted bow, because here I come, with my hair scraped into a rough bun, a milk-stained blouse, a baby in a sling, a toddler in a buggy, a nappy-bag spewing books, and what could only be described as a dangerous light in my eyes. I know that I have a six-minute window at best before the screeching begins, so I am unclipping the buggy, fast, faster now, and urging the toddler upstairs. 'No stopping.' I peek into the sling where tiny eyelids swipe in sleep, plonk the toddler by my feet and – eyes darting around in search of the librarian who once chastised me – I shove a forbidden banana into his fist. 'Please,' I whisper, 'please, just sit still while Mammy just – just –?' I tug a wrinkled list from the nappy-bag, my fingertips racing the spines. *Just two minutes*, I think, *just two*. The sling squirms and the baby rips an extravagant blast into his nappy. I smile (how could I not?), and yank the last two books from the shelf. I am grinning as I kiss the toddler's hair, grinning as I hoist my load sideways, step by slow step down the stairs, with one gooey banana-hand in mine, and a very familiar smell rising from the sling.

This is how a woman in my situation comes to chase down every translation of Eibhlín Dubh's words, of which there are many, necessitating many such library visits. Such is the number of individuals who have chosen to translate this poem that it seems almost like a rite of passage, or a series of cover-versions of a beloved old song. Many of the translations I find feeble – dead texts that try, but fail, to find the thumping pulse of Eibhlín Dubh's presence – but some are memorably strong. Few come close enough to her voice to satiate me, and the accompanying pages of her broader circumstances are often so sparse that they leave me hungry. Not just hungry. I am starving. I long to know more of her life, both before and after the moment of composition. I want to know who she was, where she came from, and what happened next. I want to know what became of her children and grandchildren. I want to read details of her burial place so I can lay flowers on her grave. I want to know her, and to know her life, and I am lazy, so I want to find all these answers laid out easily before me, preferably in a single library book. The literature available to me, however, is mostly uninterested in answering such peripheral curiosities. Still, I search, because I am convinced that there must be a text in existence, somewhere, that shares my wonder.

Once I exhaust the public libraries, I set to asking favours of university friends, stealing into libraries under assumed identities to make stealth-copies of various histories, volumes on translation, and journal articles, each source adding a brushstroke or two to the portrait of Eibhlín Dubh that is growing in my mind. I use them to add new words to my stashes of information, tucking copies under our bed, in the car, and by the breast-pump. My weeks are decanted between the twin forces of milk and text, weeks that soon pour into months, and then into years. I make myself a life in which whenever I let myself sit, it is to emit pale syllables of milk, while sipping my own dark sustenance from ink.

2. a liquid echo

go ngeobhainn é im'thaobh dheas
nó i mbinn mo léine,
is go léigfinn cead slé' leat

I'd have seized it here in my right side,
or here, in my blouse's pleats, anything,
anything to let you gallop free

—Eibhlín Dubh Ní Chonaill

I SKITTER THROUGH chaotic mornings of laundry and
lunchboxes and immunisations, always anticipating
my next session at the breast-pump, because this is
as close as I get to a rest. To sit and read while bound
to my insatiable machine is to leave my lists behind
and stroll instead through doors opened by Eibhlín
Dubh. Reading balances the strange equation of such
moments – it always feels pleasing to sit and give a
little more of myself away, especially if I can simultaneously take in a little more of her life. Once the
receptacle grows itself a liquid lid, I switch off the

pump, mark my page, then sigh and set to work again. I lift the pump to the worktop, tap the last droplets into a sterile bottle, screw the cap tightly, and write the label by hand: DOIREANN NÍ GHRÍOFA – 03/10/2012 – 250 ml.

It was through a mother-and-baby group that I first heard of the milk bank. When I googled it, I read that the stomachs of premature babies are tiny and delicate, and that exposure to formula milk may result in gut problems like necrotising enterocolitis or cardiovascular collapse. Sometimes, I read, the trauma of a premature birth can diminish a mother's supply, leaving her with little or no breastmilk to feed her baby. It was impossible to read of those horrors without making contact with the bank myself. The necessary fastidiousness of the routines came to assume a pleasing importance in my days: the sterilisation, the suds and the steam, the scrubbed skin, the pristine engine. I knew that my milk would soon be absorbed by premature and sick infants, so I was always particularly careful to maintain optimal conditions, chilling each bottle in the fridge before freezing it.

Now, I check the readout from my freezer thermometer and note the digits carefully, initial my chart, then settle the newly cooled bottle alongside eight identical bricks in the freezer, the yield of a good week. At a certain time every morning, my kitchen resembles a lab – here is the temperature chart, here, the steriliser spewing steam, here, the dismantled components of my machine, here, the tired woman, and here, the line of sterile containers. Here, every day is the same.

Once the freezer is so full that I have to wrestle a bag of peas to fit it in, I ring the milk bank at Irvinestown, and they send a polystyrene box so large that it fills the postman's arms. I slot in as many bottles as I can, sign the forms and tape the box shut, looping thick brown tape around the lid. Once. Twice. Now the baby must be anoraked, kissed, clipped into his buggy, and pacified with a teddy. His brother must be enticed away from a Duplo tower, zipped into his coat, and offered the bribe of a lollipop to coax him into town. The box is both bulky and heavy, so the only way I can carry it is by perching it above the buggy handles, balanced clumsily between chin and elbow while straining to hold the toddler's hand too. It takes twenty minutes to negotiate what is other-wise a ten-minute walk to the post office. The ordeal leaves me exasperated in the queue, promising myself that I will ask my husband to post the box next time.

At the counter, I find my favourite postman behind the glass. I've grown fond of his fuzzy grey hair, his wonky glasses, his nicotine smile, and how he always calls me *love*. He comes to the side door and I watch him stamp labels on the parcel – *Express Post, Next Day Delivery*. He passes me a receipt for reimbursement of postage costs, the sole exchange of money involved in these transactions.

I will never suckle the distant baby who will be next to swallow my milk, nor will I ever nestle his warm limbs close, but I do know the path my milk will follow on its way to him. I've googled Irvinestown, County Fermanagh, to see the village with its pretty park, three schools, a pub called *The Necarne Arms* and a chipper called *Joe 90s*. In a neat terrace, among boutiques and a hair salon, a discreet sign indicates the NHS's Western Trust Human Milk Bank. Here, my box of bottles will make its tiny contribution towards the many litres of human milk sterilised, pasteurised, and dispatched to Neonatal Intensive Care Units all over the island every year: a liquid echo.

In donating my milk, I want to help families in distress, yes, an urge sparked by empathy, but I suspect that something else is also involved: an immature, westernised idea of karma. At some level, I believe that the more helpful I can be to others, the more protection I might be acquiring for my own fledgling family. In addition to this crude notion of karma, and my sympathy for imagined babies and their imagined families, there also lurks something else: an illusion of control. There is so much in my life that I cannot hope to control. I can't control all my nights of broken sleep. I can't control the terrors that my mind chooses to review just as I close my eyes – the repetitive carousel of meningitis, comas, cars swept into oceans, house fires, or paedophiles. I can't control our landlord's whims, whether – or when – his voracity might lead to us moving house again. I can't control my children's chances of securing a place in the local primary school, whose enrolment policy (like most Irish schools) is predicated upon membership of the Catholic Church. I can, however, control the ritual of milk production: the sterilisation of the bottles, the components of the pump slotted in their correct order, the painstaking necessity of record-keeping, every procedure that I choose to perform carefully and correctly.

I pay into this insurance policy every day, and once a month a note arrives, an A4 sheet of paper folded in four and decorated with Clip-Art, on which I find handwritten details of the nameless infants who received my last batch: twins whose mother suffered post-birth complications, perhaps, a tiny girl with necrotising enterocolitis, or a baby in Crumlin recovering from a heart operation. Inside the card, a number of coins are always sellotaped, precisely matching my postage costs. When I slide them into my purse, their residual stickiness makes them cling to everything, so that every time I hand one to a cashier in Aldi, or the fishmonger's stall, I remember that somewhere, a small sick baby has my milk in his mouth. I have turned myself into a wet nurse, my connection with strangers' infants mediated by machines, by engines, and by distance.

My months fill themselves with milk and laundry and dishes, with nursery rhymes and bedtime stories, with split grocery bags, dented tins, birthday parties, hangovers, and bills. I coax many small joys from my world: clean sheets snapping on the line, laughing myself breathless in the arms of my husband, a garden slide bought for a song from the classifieds, a picnic on the beach, three small heads of hair washed to a shine, shopping list after completed shopping list – *tick, tick, tick* – all my minuscule victories.

Every day I battle entropy, tidying dropped toys and muck-elbowed hoodies, sweeping up every spiral of fallen pasta and every flung crust, scrubbing stains and dishes until no trace remains of the forces that moved through these rooms. Every hour brings with it a new permutation of the same old mess. I sweep. I wash. I tidy. I am one of The Many whose working day does not have a clocking-out time. Anyone whose days revolve around domestic work knows the satis-faction that can be found in such labour, in defining and listing the numerous components of a mess, each easily resolved by a series of well-defined manoeuvres. There is a peculiar contentment to be found in absenting oneself like this, subsumed in the needs of others: in such erasure, for me, lies joy. I make myself so busy chasing lists that I never need to look beyond the rooms through which I hurry. A child's *sorry* smile as vanilla gloop seeps into the carpet sends me running for the scrubbing cloth. Night fevers shake me from sleep to sprint for thermometer and medicine. As soon as my children wander away to play elsewhere, I scurry in to scoop up their blocks. I don't examine the face reflected in the mirrors I polish so hastily. As I clean, my labour makes of itself an invisibility. If each day is a cluttered page, then I spend my hours scrubbing its letters. In this, my work is a deletion of a presence.

—

My third son begins to walk, begins to talk, and I continue to dash through my hours, singing to him over a shoulder while distracted by the stewardship of another load of laundry, by typing new poems, clearing out cupboards, or kissing his brother's bumped head. The milk bank prefers donations from mothers of younger babies, so I slowly reduce my time at the pump until I could post my final box. *Tick*.

Once the burden on my breasts diminishes, my inner clockwork clicks back to its usual configuration, bringing with it a hormonal swerve I hadn't expected. Desire returns, slamming open the door. Desire flings me to my knees, makes me tremble and beg, makes me crawl and gasp in the dark. Desire leaves me sprawled over beds and over tables, animal, throbbing, and wet. Every time I come, I weep. I missed it, desire, blissful and ordinary. I can't remember a time when I felt so relieved, or so happy.

Too soon, the landlord makes it known that a relative requires a place to live, and sends us on our way with yet another exceptional reference. I set to work immediately, finding what will become our fifth home in as many years. Weeks after we move out, a friend sees our old house advertised online at a much higher rent. I don't care. I find myself pregnant again, joyful and dusting, painting and decluttering. I can't imagine how, with four children under six, I will find time to brush my teeth, to read old poems or drink my morning tea, let alone donate milk to the babies of strangers. Twice, I lift my bag of pumping para-phernalia and consider giving it away.

Twice I put it back again.

Just in case.

—

In choosing to carry a pregnancy, a woman gives of her body with a selflessness so ordinary that it goes unnoticed, even by herself. Her body becomes bound to altruism as instinctively as to hunger. If she cannot consume sufficient calcium, for example, that mineral will rise up from deep within her bones and donate itself to her infant on her behalf, leaving her own system in deficiency. Sometimes a female body serves another by effecting a theft upon itself.

3. to breathe elsewhere

chuiris parlús á ghealadh dhom,

for you set a parlour gleaming for me,

—Eibhlín Dubh Ní Chonaill

A BODY HOLDS SO MUCH beyond the visible. Before it was ever transcribed or translated, *Caoineadh Airt Uí Laoghaire* was preserved in oral folklore, reverberating through a succession of female bodies, from female mouth to female ear, over years and years and years. Decades after its composition, it shifted through bodies again, this time from voice to hand to paper, and eventually into the literary canon. In Peter Levi's inaugural address as Oxford Professor of Poetry, he called it the 'greatest poem written in these islands in the whole eighteenth century'. What is it about this poem that evokes such passionate pronouncements, and such devotion?

I know I should be grateful to the many transla-
tors and scholars who have lent their time to Eibhlín
Dubh's work – if it weren't for such acts of attention, her words may never have reached me – but a
selfish part of me itches to despise them, and to curse
their rickety translations. Having listened to every
cover version, not only do I feel certain that no one
could ever be as devoted to her as I am, but I find
myself wanting to sing, too. I know how unquali-
fied I am to attempt my own translation – I hold
no doctorate, no professorship, no permission-slip
at all – I am merely a woman who loves this poem.
The task of translation itself, however, does not feel
unfamiliar to me, not only due to translating my
own poems, but because the process feels so close
to homemaking. In Italian, the word *stanza* means
'room'. If there are times when I feel ill-equipped and
daunted by the expertise of those who have walked
these rooms before me, I reassure myself that I am
simply homemaking, and this thought steadies me,
because tending to a room is a form of labour I know
that I can attempt as well as anyone.

In the small gap between dinner and the children's bedtime, my husband clears the table while
I rush upstairs, taking the steps two by two, leaving
my own home behind in order to hoist myself into
that of a stranger. I snap open my laptop, tip-tap the

document in which Eibhlín Dubh's words wait, and hurry through the door of a new stanza, measuring furniture and carpets, feeling the textures of fabrics between thumb and finger, and testing their weight. Then I set to replication. If I am to conjure her presence, I must first construct a suitable home for her, building and furnishing room after careful room, in which each mirror will catch her reflection.

As soon as I finish the first verse, I step back to admire the room I have conjured. Despite my best efforts, the door won't shut properly and the floorboards are so uneven that a reader could suffer a splinter if they were to enter in bare feet. Regardless, the first verse is complete. Thirty-five more remain. My translation begins as it will continue: it is far from flawless, but it is mine. I feel confident, as I assess this first imperfect stanza, that I will not regret taking on this work. The following evening, I turn to the second verse and take it as a good omen when I find the opening phrase 'Is domhsa nárbh aithreach', or 'And never did I regret it'. This verse builds into a list that details how Art prepared a marital home for Eibhlín Dubh:

> for you set a parlour gleaming for me,
> bedchambers brightened for me,
> an oven warming for me,
> plump loaves rising for me,

meats twisting on spits for me,
beef butchered for me,
and duck-down slumbers for me
until midday-milking, or beyond
if I'd want.

In every translated line of this verse, I feel that I am mimicking the homemaking actions of centuries before, stuffing quilts with duck-feathers, painting walls and kneading dough. For months I work methodically, deliberating between synonyms, stitching and re-stitching the seams of curtains until they fall just so, letting my eye move back and forth between verbs, straightening the rugs, and polishing each linguistic ornament. Like my housework, the results of my translation are often imperfect, despite my devotion. I forget to swipe the hoover under a chair, or I spend hours washing windows and still leave smears. I often ignore cobwebs. I often stumble. I continue anyway. This work allows me a sense of purpose for many beautiful verses, and many absorbing months. As I approach the end of the poem, however, I feel something close to dread. I don't want it to to end.

In attending so closely to Eibhlín Dubh's words, I have come to know her speech in ways I couldn't possibly have otherwise. Such a methodical undertaking requires a deliberation, a decelerated reading, and a kind of repetitive looping: back, and back, and back again. I have spent hours frowning at my screen, struggling against myself as I try to capture a phrase of hers and re-create it within the strictures of another language. Such dedication, if nothing else, has permitted me to grow in slow intimacy with the poet herself, to discover the particular swerve of her thoughts and the pulse of her language. I am saddened to leave Eibhlín's rooms behind, and saddened to omit her name from my lists. Even when I know for sure that my translation is finished, I often return to visit – straightening the angle of a mirror here, polishing an empty brass keyhole there – but despite my pains over each syllable and verse, despite my conscientiousness in the pursuit of fidelity, my finished text feels slight to me, as lopsided and as flawed as myself. I have grown fond of my translation, but this fondness, I know, is rooted in the twin intimacies of familiarity and closeness, rather than in artistic satisfaction. I slam the laptop shut and run downstairs to sob to my husband that my attempt has failed in all the same ways as the other translations I've been complaining about. Mine, like theirs, has not come close to the timbre of her voice – or at least, not as close as I had hoped. He wraps his arms around me.

My document doesn't hold her voice and as such, I judge it a failure – an inevitable failure, but a failure nonetheless. I try to accept this fact while showing myself compassion. I have gained so much from my work. For one thing, I have learned that the element I cherish most of all in Eibhlín Dubh's work does not lie in any of the rooms I spent hours deliberating over. No, my favourite element hovers beyond the text, in the untranslatable pale space between stanzas, where I sense a female breath lingering on the stairs, still present, somehow, long after the body has hurried onwards to breathe elsewhere. If I have left something of myself within this translation, it is only the weary sigh that leaves my lungs when, at last, I make myself close the document and move on.

4. in the milking parlour

Do bhuaileas go luath mo bhasa
is do bhaineas as na reathaibh

Fast, I clapped my hands,
and fast, fast, I galloped,

—Eibhlín Dubh Ní Chonaill

A FAMILY CALENDAR scrawled with biro and pencil marks, each in the same hand – this is a female text. Month after month after month of appointments, swim lessons, half-days, bake sales, fundraisers, library returns, a baby's due-date, birthday parties, and school holidays. *Tick. Tick. Tick.* Each November, I choose a new calendar from the supermarket. By January, the old one will be added to the stack: these are my sweetest years, archived in paper and ink, in white and black.

2012.

2013.

2014.

2015

At 7.46 AM on a Tuesday in June, an ultrasound wand slithers the slope of my belly. It dawdles, then slowly reverses. The slower the wand, the faster my pulse; it speeds from canter to gallop as I lift my head to watch the wand move slower still. Slower. Slower. Stop.

The consultant is ringing the maternity hospital even as I scoop her gel from my bellybutton, negotiating how soon she can arrange a caesarean section. Although only one side of the conversation is audible, my muscular sense of dread soon sets to filling the gaps. Hanging up the phone, she explains that she has seen a number of calcifications on my placenta, white blotches that indicate the occurrence of infarcts, or strokes. In these areas, the placental tissue has died and is incapable of sustaining a baby who is now much, much smaller than anticipated, and struggling to survive in decreased amniotic fluid. A baby. My baby.

I find myself in the hospital soon afterwards. I must have driven myself but I don't recall the journey. A nurse tugs down my leggings and stabs my buttock with steroid injections, hoping to hasten the baby's lungs. I am given an arrival time for a C-section the following day. If I notice any change in the baby's movements, they say, any change at all, I am to rush

straight in from home – no waiting room, no checking
at reception, 'Just run past security and straight to
the midwives' station.' 'But they'll stop me,' I say,
laughing. My laugh is not returned.

'No they won't, they'll know.'

'Should I show them my file?'

'No, they'll know by your face.'

My thumb shakes when I text my husband to tell
him what has happened, wanting to reassure him, as
I reassure myself, as I attempt to reassure you now in
your distance. I write 'everything's ok. baby will come
maybe tomorrow. off to the shops for a few things.'
Then I text my mum, 'Can you come to mind the
boys? Dr thinks baby might come soon. xx' Each
message I send takes the information I have been given
and communicates an impression that allows me to
loiter safely around Penneys for ten minutes, because
nothing can truly be wrong if I am ambling through
racks of cartoon slippers and hoodies, my fingers idly
patting layers of fleece and lace and brushed cotton
pyjamas. My phone beeps in reply with the wordless
dots, dashes, and ellipses of grinning text-faces. The
baby is quiet as I stroll the aisles, and I imagine it
snoozing, lulled by my momentum.

At home, I tell my husband that it could all be a fuss
over nothing, smiling and shoving him out the door
and back to a factory where phones are prohibited. He

believes me; I believe myself. I set to my chores. If I am washing dishes, everything must be fine. If I am scrubbing scrambled egg from a pot, everything must be fine. My friend Amy rings and I try to convince her that 'yeah, I'm definitely fine'. If I am hanging wet clothes in the sun, that means everything is fine, doesn't it? I hoover the sitting room, and the bodily repetition of that mundane back-and-forthing is the same as it has always been – surely nothing can go wrong in a person's life if they are hoovering. My cousin Saoirse texts: 'Baby moving?'

I reply: 'Not now but everything is fine.' Smiley face. Delete the smiley face. Delete the letters one by one. I shower and then try to blow-dry my hair, but my attention stumbles when the phone vibrates in my pocket. Saoirse again.

> Baby moving yet?
> Not now but we're fine! Just had a shower. xx
> Getting worried. When will you go in?
> Everything is ok :-)
> Call the doc! Pls!!

No matter how chirpy I try to sound, she resists my tellings, she sees right through me, and her reading of the situation is beginning to get to me. I lie on the sofa and make myself eat a Cornetto, willing the baby to squirm against the cold ice-cream, to kick in protest, as it always has. Nothing. I wait, staring at the speckled ceiling. Still nothing. It all thunders down on me and suddenly I can't breathe.

The baby is no longer moving.

The baby has stopped moving.

What the fuck am I doing?

My parents still haven't arrived, so I jostle the three boys into the car – I'll leave them with Amy. Grabbing my hospital bag, I fling my tattered photocopy of the *Caoineadh* in too, then accelerate through the estate in tears, trying to hide my face from the children.

A small dog is sauntering along the road. I brake and ask some passing teenagers to hold him for a minute. They grab his collar and pet his soft head. *There.* Everything is fine, everything is under control. I accelerate, and, in every one of my vertebrae, I feel the wheels run over the dog. In the mirror the teen-agers are hurrying towards his crumpled body, but I am still driving. I haven't stopped. Why haven't I stopped? My children ask, 'What was that sound?' 'Nothing,' I lie. The eldest looks out the back window, and the youngest asks, 'Will you bring the doggy to the hospital too?' 'I'll come back for him later,' I say. 'Why are you crying?' 'No, not crying. I'm fine.' I imagine dog blood on the wheels. I imagine brains. Mush. My baby is not moving. My breath comes rough and jagged, my throat hurts. I lift the children from the car to Amy, haul their car seats out, and point my car towards the maternity hospital. Alone, I howl.

The baby still won't move. What can I put right? I return to our housing estate and drive around until I find the teenagers. They point me towards its owner's house. I am a mess. The baby still isn't moving, but 'the dog is fine' she says, gesturing towards a basket whose occupant holds a paw to me with sad eyes. I cry. The woman shoos me to the hospital.

—

The journey along the motorway unspools itself fast, so fast that even the furze turns blurred and reckless. I park my car at a wonky angle and run, wheezing through the corridors. Every security guard, every nurse and patient I encounter steps aside. I am soon hooked to machines, watching a long paper scroll unravelling under the machine's finger, scraping a story of struggle and fall. The curtain tugged around my bed is a flimsy boundary, and though I can't make out their words, I guess the nurses are talking about me, as the rhythm of their female voices reveals concern. I long for my husband. I want to see him more than anyone. My finger shakes as I text him: 'Don't panic but I am in hospital. Come quick.'

Hours pass.

No movement.

Then, a weak kick. My husband arrives in his motorbike pants, helmet under his elbow. I am unspeakably relieved to see him. 'Everything's OK,' I say, 'I have it under control.'

—

The nurses prepare me for the first C-section of a new day. Many people enter the room in scrubs, speaking to each other urgently. The anaesthetist checks that my legs have gone numb. My doctor enters, warm and reassuring, eyes smiling over her mask. A sheet is raised between us. I imagine the blade held over my body for one trembling moment. Then, she brings it down. She cuts me open. My husband presses his lips to my hand, and holds my gaze. Beyond the sheet, there is much tugging and pulling, a sudden sensation of pressure, of lift, followed by a weird lightness. The sheet is lowered. I watch the baby emerge from my body.

I see her, a girl. A tiny girl.

I am so fuzzy with spinal morphine, with joy, excitement and adrenaline, that her extreme smallness doesn't seem frightening at all. She looks perfect to me. She is lifted quickly to an incubator at the far end of the room, where a huddle of doctors begin to work on her. The smell of barbecue, of burning, I realise slowly, is me: it is coming from my body. The consultant smiles as she works, says how glad she is to have gotten my daughter out when she did, that things were far worse within than she could have imagined from the scan. My baby had not grown in weeks, and both placenta and umbilical cord had failed to such an extent that that she would have been stillborn had she waited any longer. I can think of nothing to say in response. I try to smile. My daughter is here, and she is alive – I hear her mewling from the corner.

In the recovery room, the baby's eyes open when she latches to my breast and sucks fiercely. A new doctor introduces himself and insists that she be given a bottle of formula. I grin tightly. I refuse. 'None of my children has ever been given artificial milk,' I say, 'and anyway, she will be fine, everything is fine now.' The doctor grows cold and strong: this is not a suggestion, it is a necessity. My calcified placenta had failed to provide the baby with sufficient nutrition; this is why her movements slowed. The doctors now suspect that her blood sugar levels might be worryingly low; a test before and after the consumption of a specific volume of milk would allow them to confirm whether her body is capable of processing sugars efficiently. The output of my

breasts cannot be calibrated, so they need to feed
her a bottle immediately. I nod, and then I watch
my daughter feed in the arms of a stranger; my baby,
holding a plastic nipple between her tiny lips. I
laugh at how easy it is, and how uncanny. My world
feels slightly askew, surreal and yet eerily normal –
like one of those old sitcoms where characters turn
off the lights at bedtime, and suddenly everything
glows blue. We are in the same recovery room where
I lay with all my newborns, but this time it has been
cast in a different light.

The test results allow us to be wheeled to the ward
together, a small victory. Visiting hours are over, so
my husband kisses us both and heads home to put
our sons to bed. The baby sleeps and sleeps. She will
not open her eyes, let alone breastfeed. I try every
trick I remember from my other babies: stroking her
cheek with damp cotton wool, blowing on her belly,
tickling. I hum the same tune I hummed to my sons:
'I've given all I can, it's not enough, I've given all I can.'
Still she won't wake.

I start to panic, though I am determined to hide
my fear from the doctors who want to take her from
me. They grow exasperated at my insistence that
everything is fine, that breastfeeding will settle down
eventually. They want her in an environment where
they can monitor her blood continuously. If I can

hand-express a certain amount of milk and feed it to her by syringe, they will allow us another few hours to show an improvement in her blood tests. If that happens, they will let her remain with me. If not, well … The threat dangles. *So*, I think, *the test I must pass to keep her with me is to express breast milk? Easy.* I ask for paper, a pen, and some bottles. I begin to hand-express, squeezing bright yellow colostrum from my breasts, drop by slow drop. I try to remember to note the night feeds, so I can prove to the doctors how well she fed – efforts that leave me with the following artefact, a sad, barely legible text blurred by the dregs of morphine in my blood.

Expressed 5ml. She's asleep.

Expressed a bit more. Tried bottle but she won't wake up. Squeezing some drops directly from breast into her mouth, but it just dribbled back out. Changed babygro. Nappy a bit damp

Still adding to colostrum – plenty pumped, but her gums still clamped. How can I feed her if she won't let me?

Think I fell asleep. A few minutes anyway. Squeezed drops into her mouth again but think it all dripped out. Nothing

She stirred in her sleep and spat up. Changed Babygro. Nappy dry

Why won't she wake up??? Tried bottle again. Can't do it.

Crying now, still can't get her to drink bottle. What is wrong, her or me?

Asked new nurse for help. She got all the milk into her in no time. Sleep now. So tired

Baby just spewed. all gone. tried to feed her but gums closed. awful. changed babygro and blankets. nappy still dry.

so worried. nurse said try to wake her again soon.

expressed more. squeezed drops on her lips but don't think she swallowed much really. she won't wake. scared now

burped her and tried bottle again. failed. called midwife but no answer

can't stop crying – she's asleep, nappy bone dry – v scared, don't know what to do

nurse said she will discuss with reg. baby still asleep

nothing nothing

I don't show this page to anyone. By 3.15 AM my throat hurts again from crying in frustration. I have hand-expressed a full bottle of colostrum and watched it dribble drip by precious drip from the baby's clenched jaw. I can't get her to swallow. I am jittery now, jittery and panicking. A registrar pinpricks my daughter's foot, holds it to the electronic monitor that measures blood levels, and raises her eyebrows. Her voice is calm, but within five minutes two young doctors are wheeling my baby away. I will not be allowed to follow her until I am free of both IV and catheter.

The door closes.

I have failed. My baby has been taken from me, hurried away to breathe elsewhere. I lie staring at the wall. My milk seeps from me, unseen: a pale text in pale sheets.

—

My room is located in a ward several floors above my baby's unit, but the hospital brings her any milk I can hand-express. A poster in my room blares MOTHER'S MILK IS BEST, and yet the nurse will not let me use their breast-pumps. 'Hand expression only,' she says, in a gentle voice. I demand a second opinion, but the registrar agrees with the nurse: it is hospital policy that no woman be allowed a pump until day three after birth. When I ask why, the answer is always 'Hospital policy.' I raise my voice. I curse. I tell them that if I do not pump *now* my supply will drop and I will have no milk to feed my baby once we leave this place. I say that if they refuse I will simply send my husband home for my own pump. I make fists and hit my legs, I shake and growl, and with that they relent.

The machine, when it arrives, is unlike any pump I've ever seen. A top-of-the-range model, it is not carried, but rather wheeled in, and yet when I flick the switch, the song is the same, the old chorus of suck/hiss, suck/hiss. All it takes is a whisper of that noise and my breasts begin to weep. I wish I could say that this routine is something of a comfort. It isn't. I feel cheated and weary; I feel defeated. So many mornings spent pumping for babies in Neonatal ICUs, pitying their mothers, and now here I sit, without my baby, uselessly spilling liquid: milk into the breast-pump, urine into the catheter, while snif-fling and weeping into tissues. 'It could be worse,' the nurses say – 'you're the mum whose baby was nearly stillborn? They'll take great care of her, below. Don't you worry. Relax. Rest. Good girl.' Once everyone has left, the door closes softly. There is only one voice who never leaves my side; Eibhlín Dubh is with me, close as ink on paper and steady as a pulse.

My husband texts me photos of our daughter in her incubator, naked but for a nappy and covered in wires and tubes. This baby doesn't look like any other child of mine, she looks like one of the babies in the milk-bank leaflets. I stare at the photos, terrified.

I never remember falling asleep in my sad room, but every time I do, I am woken by the cries of infants who aren't mine. All night, they wail, the babies of strangers, all night they weep and weep into the sterile dark. Every time I jolt up to another baby's cry, I feel I've been dreaming of the same thing, I just can't ever remember what it was. Something – dark – something – ajar. Whenever I wake, I reach for the machine and pump as though I have something to prove. Nurses swoop through the corridors to arrive at my bedside with clipboards and tiny paper goblets, each filled with pain pills. *Ah*, I say, heaving myself up on my elbows. *Ah*.

Once my drip and catheter have been tugged away, I must demonstrate that I can urinate competently into a cardboard bucket. The nurse peers at my sloshing wavelets and nods. I am elated. Soon, a porter arrives with a wheelchair and I lower my sore body into its frame. He pushes me down, down, down, all the way down to the NICU.

It is only when I am finally sitting by my daughter's incubator that I begin to accept the swerve we have taken. I am not permitted to lift her without permission. Instead, I spend hours staring from beyond the glass, weeping intermittently over the fuzz of her spine, her eyelashes, her tiny hands, how grey the cheek that rests on her arm. It is dizzying to let my body express intimate fears in such a public place, but I do, I let my cries echo those of the others who are also stuck in this room, crying too. It's a chorus. I join in.

The NICU is a large, long, busy chamber in which multiple scenes are all occurring at once. To allow a weary gaze to hover there for even a moment is to find oneself a witness to any number of private human catastrophes, each in its own slow implosion. Any time I look up from the incubator, it dizzies me with its simultaneity: here, a cluster of registrars shaking their heads over a chart, there, a woman weeping beyond earshot; here, one nurse warms a bottle, there, another lifts a baby while tubes cobweb behind him; here, a father and a mother are smiling, each holding one tiny twin to the warm skin of their chests, there, three doctors shoulder through the main door; here, a man with his elbows on his knees, head in hands, strong shoulders heaving. He sobs. She sobs. We all fucking sob. Beyond his chair, three more couples sit by incubators, scrolling and swiping their phones, while a new mother limps past, rubbing disinfectant gel hand to hand. In any single moment, we are all enduring and crumpling, fighting and weeping, laughing and dozing, watching and being watched. Whether real or imagined, my sense of surveillance here is strong. I feel that I must pass some nameless test with each new professional we encounter. I'm sure that my tantrum over the breast-pump has been noted in my file, so now I try to make myself smile politely, imagining that there could be some correlation between the level of normality I can feign and how our daughter might be treated. All I want is to fling myself to my knees and beg the doctors to let me hold my daughter, but I can't do that. If we are to take her home, I must both control myself and relinquish control to them.

Within the ward, I am shown to a smaller, narrower room with cold leather sofas, a sink, a fridge, a TV, and a row of breast-pumps. The nurse calls it 'the milking parlour'. Beyond its door, I find the other mothers: the blonde teenager in a Snoopy nightie, the teacher with pearls in her earlobes, the farmer, the smoker, and all the others. Every two hours, we leave our incubator vigils and hook ourselves up to the machines, watching afternoon repeats of *EastEnders* and *Room to Improve* and discussing the merits of galactagogues: oats, fenugreek, and dandelion tea. We pass the stories of each new horror in hurried whispers, mouth to ear to mouth to ear. The stories we tell are inoculations, repeated in the unconscious hope that they might protect our own babies from sharing the same fates. No logic attaches itself to this impulse, just as little logic seems to attach itself to the cruelties that are being inflicted on our infants. In this room, we laugh more than we cry, but we are all exhausted and terrified. One woman wears a niqāb, the rest of us are in pyjamas and slippers, and we are all in hell together.

The unit is organised according to the severity of each baby's condition. My daughter starts on C Wall, where babies are sometimes discharged within hours of arrival. I spend all our time on C Wall yearning to carry her back to the maternity floor with me, thinking that we could be given permission to do so at any moment. When she is moved to A Wall I daydream about bringing her back to C Wall. On their rounds, the doctors discuss her most recent bloods and tinker with her glucose drip. I hold my husband's hand tight. Our baby is so weak that she doesn't cry, no matter how often the nurses poke her heel with their tiny blade. I live for the times when I am allowed to nestle her to my breast in weary bliss. I press my lips to her heels when the tests make her bleed, my mouth tidying droplets of blood until her skin is clean.

Although she is kept at the A Wall, I feel lucky. Her endocrine problems may be complex, but the doctor's treatment plan seems straightforward by comparison with the stories I hear in the milking parlour. Some days are dark, the doctors' reports delivered with shakes of the head. On others, we feel sure that somehow, some day, we will leave the NICU. When she is strong, she feeds from my breast, but when she is weak, my milk comes to her by tube, by syringe or by bottle. I go to the milking parlour every couple of hours, not only to keep a supply of my milk available, but also because it's the only thing I can do that feels useful. Whenever my breasts tingle, I tuck some words between elbow and rib and slipper-shuffle back to that narrow room again. There, I pump and read as I always did at home, and some-times it feels almost normal. I slide my bottles into the fridge alongside those sent by the milk bank, each with their neatly handwritten labels, each bearing the names of strangers.

Time veers weirdly in the NICU. The ordering of events seems to blur and rumple unexpectedly. I get so little sleep. I hurt myself. I fall against a wall, crashing my head into a corner, or tumble into a door as it slams on my shoulder. My body develops its own account of these weeks, a vocabulary of bruises, aching breasts, dressings, stitchings, and a slow, tender limp.

One afternoon, my parents visit the glass door of the emergency exit next to our incubator, and one by one, they lift my sons up. I miss them so much. While the boys blow kisses to their tiny, sleeping sister, I turn my wet face away. Through this same glass door, I have seen a bird fluttering over the slip-road to land on the branch of a young tree. I have watched an ambulance freewheel silently towards the garage. Twice, I have seen a hearse there, its wheels turning slowly over its own shadow.

I grow fond of the cleaners in their pristine smocks, the choreography of their homely routines: the swift swirl of an industrial mop, the smile, the cloth-rub, the nod. I learn their names and their idiosyncrasies – who swipes the light switch before the filing cabinet, who makes eye-contact, who tells a joke, whose gaze clings respectfully to the floor when they find me snivelling again. I grow homesick, watching the dance of their cleaning; I ache for my washing machine, my broom, the *tick* of my kitchen clock, the *tick-tick* of my lists. No day here is predictable, no day is the same. I fret over what will happen next; I fret and fret and try to force myself to relax into the dread, but nothing here makes sense. Everything I see seems to be occurring in a rush, both too close and at a great distance from me. One afternoon, on my way to the bathroom, I see a teenage boy follow his partner's wheelchair into the unit. She is very pale under her freckles. A nurse hugs her. Behind them, the baby is wheeled in by a group of doctors, followed soon afterwards by a priest. The room grows silent around them – or maybe I imagine that. By the time I return, they are all gone, and the NICU is bustling as usual.

—

I grow angry whenever nurses ask me to leave. Shortly before any procedure, they arrive, gesturing towards the corridor. When I grow vexed, sighing rowdily, they insist, and if I have learned anything about myself here, it is that I am weak. I always relent. On a leather sofa in the corridor, I sit and glare like a child until finally they invite me back to find a new dressing covering a new wound. I loathe them for making my baby and I suffer alone, when I know I should be by her side.

One afternoon, I witness this same choreography played out with the family who sit at the incubator opposite ours, the parents shaking their heads to the spread fingers of the nurse, her tilted head, coaxing, coaxing softly, and eventually, their resentful departure. I recognise the father's tight fists behind his back. After they leave, I watch a screen assembled around their baby, a boundary intended to generate an illusion of privacy. The screen cannot mute the infant's screams, however, nor can it block the song of the nurses who stroke its brow, who coo as they hold it still for whatever agonies of syringe or cold scalpel that follow. This tiny howl is a sound I will never excise from my memory. I weep as I listen – I weep in helplessness, yes, but I also weep in gratitude for those nurses' certainty that parents must spare themselves from witnessing a child's agonies. The nurse insists. The nurse stands in their place.

—

In the milking parlour, the conversation loops around and around and around. It is a room bound by spilled secrets and fear, a room that exists in a spiral of its own repetitions: bleeding nipples, murmurs, infected wounds, heart operations, dwindling yields, surgeries, unexplained pains, referrals, queried clots, the list goes on and on and on. Hope. Home. Meningitis. Crumlin. Home. Coma. Home. Home. Home.

Whenever a baby does go home, I watch the mother carefully. On entering the milking parlour to say goodbye, her face reveals a muddle of relief mixed with pity for those of us who have to stay. I am glad for them, and yet these moments always feel like a betrayal. A childish part of me wants to keep everything here the same. When new mothers arrive, we show them how to use the pumps and where to store their milk. We listen to their stories. We pass them tissues. We say the magic words, we tell them that *everything will be OK*. We pat their hands. We smile. We know, unequivocally, that everything will not be OK, at least not until they can escape this place, but such is the script of this room, and we adhere to it loyally. These weeks teach me this performance, just as they teach me to sleep in a chair, my head lolling and falling, my gaze faltering between glaring fluorescence and the warm dark of elsewheres.

—

One morning, a consultant holds my daughter's chart aloft and announces that today is our day. He utters the word I have yearned to hear. *Home.* I am so joyful that I cannot speak. I grip both his hands in mine and nod and nod, I hold tight until his gaze falls to the floor and his jaw grows hard, and still I thank him, still I grip and grip, so afraid am I to let go. If I do, he might change his mind. I grip him because some strange part of me is afraid of walking away, and that part of me wants to stay. Here, my daughter is safe, monitored by machines and by professionals, but at home there will be only me. Only me. I may be relieved to return home, but I am also terrified of leaving this ghastly familiarity. Even horror can be homely. The consultant watches all this play across my face in silence, then tugs his hands away, and pats me firmly on the shoulder. 'Everything will be OK,' he says.

My hands shake a little as I clear cupboards of our nappies, babygros, and blankets, the crumpled coffee cups, my photocopy of the *Caoineadh*, and my stack of long-overdue library books. I wiggle my daughter's hand in a wave goodbye. Finally, I will bring her outside.

At the last minute, I remember my shelf in the milking parlour and hurry back to grab a plastic bag and fling in all of my own cold milk. So many bottles peer back from that dark – among them, those of the milk bank – as ready as ghosts, pale and prepared. I close the door. I walk away.

5. an unscientific mishmash

mar a bhfásaid caora
is cnó buí ar ghéagaibh
is úlla 'na slaodaibh
na n-am féinig.

where sheep grow plump, and branches
grow heavy with clusters of nuts,
where apples spill lush
when their sweet season rises up.

—Eibhlín Dubh Ní Chonaill

IN THE WEEKS AFTER the baby comes home from the hospital, all my old routines return, preventing me from dwelling too much on the strange weeks that followed the birth. I am gladder than ever of my lists and the daily chores with which I fill them: the hoovering, the groceries, the baths, and the laundry. It is an anchoring, the simple joy of drawing a line through a task. Whenever my daughter settles into my elbow to feed, I reach for a book. Through scholarly volumes, through histories of eighteenth-century Ireland, through translations and old maps, I continue to find all the information I can on Eibhlín Dubh's life, no matter how obscure or tangential. The more I read, the more my folder of notes grows.

In the months after my daughter is born the act of reciting the *Caoineadh* comes to feel like time-travel – I am carrying this baby in the same sling and whispering the same verses as I did with her brother. When her sleeping ear rests against my chest, it reverberates with Eibhlín Dubh's words. What dreams might she spin from these whisperings? What galloping hooves? What howls?

—

The public health nurse arranges a home visit and I lose myself in scrubbing, my mind whirling around the dread that she'll point to some stray cobweb or juice spillage as evidence to remove my children. My palms are slick, watching her set her scales on our kitchen table. She asks for tea, and I curse myself silently for not having a pot ready. By the time I return with our best chipped cups, she is leafing through my folder. I want to dive across the table, growling *No! Mine!* Instead, I pour her tea and try to smile. She laughs at herself, tapping the page. 'Art O'Leary! Probably as close as we got to boy-bands, in my day.' I try to mask my grimace.

While she reminisces about her school days, I let my tired gaze drift to my teacup, how it curves like an ear, embellished with twists of blue. I think of the gesture a cup demands, the tilt towards a mouth, the flow. My eye translates the image on the cup and I flinch. How have I not noticed this? For years, I've been drinking from a cup of starlings. I think of their song, how deftly they regurgitate strands of true, remembered sound, weaving it into their own melodic bridges: a fusion of truth and invention, of past and present. The expectant silence that always follows a query drags me back to the nurse, who has paused her finger in its trespass of my scribblings and is peering at me. She repeats her question. 'Taking a night course, are we?' I shake my head. 'So what's all this for, then?' My shoulders answer on my behalf, my whole body pickling crimson. She soon turns to scolding me about the baby instead: no feeding schedule, no set sleep routine, one would imagine with a fourth child a mother would be a little more, well … she lifts her brows and palms.

After she leaves I weep, more in rage than in shame, her words lingering: *So what's all this for, then?*

—

I don't know what it's all for, but I keep going anyway, in the misguided hope that if I can simply exhaust my obsession it might come to bore me, eventually. It's a foolish approach that only makes things worse, because the more I read, the sharper my rage grows. This feeling glues itself to the introductory paragraph that often precedes the translations, flimsy sketches of Eibhlín Dubh's life that are almost always some lazy variant of the same two facts: *Wife of Art O'Leary. Aunt of Daniel O'Connell.* How swiftly the academic gaze places her in a masculine shadow, as though she could only be of interest as a satellite to male lives.

In my anger, I begin to sense some project that might answer the nurse's query. Perhaps I'd always known what it was all for. Perhaps I'd stumbled upon my true work. Perhaps the years I'd spent sifting the scattered pieces of this jigsaw were not in vain; perhaps they were a preparation. Perhaps I could honour Eibhlín Dubh's life by building a truer image of her days, gathering every fact we hold to create a kaleidoscope, a spill of distinct moments, fractured but vivid. Once this thought comes to me, my heart grows quick. *I could donate my days to finding hers,* I tell myself, *I could do that, and I will.*

—

I begin with an unscientific mishmash of daydream and fact, concocted while scraping porridge gloop into a bin, gathering schoolbags and coats, badgering children into the car, biting back curses at traffic lights, kissing three boys goodbye, and driving back home again. All the while, I keep one eye on Eibhlín Dubh and one on my daughter in her car seat. She grows in that rear-view mirror. Soon, her eyes are open as I turn towards home. Soon, her gurgles can almost be translated into words. Soon, she is tugging at the straps in which I have bound her. Soon, she is smiling back at me. This is how years pass in that mirror: soon, too soon.

One morning, at 9:23 AM, I pause at the school gates. Instead of turning left towards home and its basketful of ironing, I turn right, my fingers wandering radio stations as I drive. A former taoiseach has died, and his achievements are repeated through the fond, caramel nostalgia of men: *A great man. Ah, a great man.* I push the dial to silence. Now only three voices are borne along our path of bitumen and asphalt, and all three are female: mine, my daughter's, and that of the GPS who guides us towards Kilcrea in a tone that is flatly authoritative. [Turn Left] she directs, her voice scoured clean of social expectation.

We are lifted over the river by a bridge so narrow that it sings less of engines and more of hooves. I open our windows and cut the engine. Birdsong flutters in. It may be late October, but the trees here are still deeply leaved, singing richly in the breeze, exactly as trees sang when Eibhlín Dubh approached this place. Goosebumps punctuate my skin. She was here. A horse carried her across this bridge, over the river Bride. *Betrothed. Bríd.* Soon she will meet the river Lee, her name will change, and she will become something else, but for now, this little river lingers under the trees, humming her own liquid melodies.

Beyond the bridge, the abbey rises from a patchwork of fields, warm and wormy under an unseasonably cloudless sky. My daughter smiles. She is wearing a bright pink cardigan knitted by her grandmother, a female text in which every stitch is a syllable. I lift her, along with my bag, my phone, my notebook, pen, and camera, and shuffle through the stile sideways. This is the life I have made for myself, always striving for something beyond my grasp, while hauling implausibly complex armfuls.

Walking the neat avenue towards the abbey, I remember that Eibhlín Dubh, in walking this same path, would have found it bordered by bone. In 1774, Charles Smith documented his travels here in

The Ancient and Present State of the County and City of Cork. Arriving at the approach to this abbey, he describes 'high banks on either side, formed entirely of human bones and skulls, cemented together with moss; and besides great numbers strown about, there are several thousands piled up in the arches, windows, &c.' All those bones have been neatly tidied into the ground in the meantime; the only skulls beyond the soil now are ours and those of the crows.

'Kilcrea' means 'the church of Créidh', after the first abbess to establish a holy house here. Later, monks built a celebrated monastery on this same site, sturdy stone walls against which their devotion would ricochet, while later still, in another time, to another tune, Eibhlín Dubh spoke her grief in their ruins. Now, autumn comes and brings me with it, drawn by a motive I can't quite explain, even to myself. Perhaps this pilgrimage is my first step towards her. I walk, and as I walk, my heels imprint themselves in the dirt, adding another line to its old ledger of footprints. Within, I arrange my body as I imagine others held theirs – I look up.

Above is the scriptorium where monks bent over a table, filling the air with the steady scrape of quill on vellum. Careful, careful replications: oh, the serious labours of man. Back then, poems were traditionally commissioned by *taoisigh* – leaders of the old Gaelic order – who would employ a (male) bard to commemorate a person or an event in verse. These poems were copied into *duanairí*, handwritten anthologies that often also held genealogies and sacred texts. By contrast, literature composed by women was stored not in books but in female bodies, living repositories of poetry and song. I have come across a line of argument in my reading, which posits that, due to the inherent fallibility of memory and the imperfect human vessels that held it, the *Caoineadh* cannot be considered a work of single authorship. Rather, the theory goes, it must be considered collage, or, perhaps, a folky reworking of older keens. This, to me – in the brazen audacity of one positioned far from the tall walls of the university – feels like a male assertion pressed upon a female text. After all, the etymology of the word 'text' lies in the Latin verb 'texere': to weave, to fuse, to braid. The *Caoineadh* form belongs to a literary genre worked and woven by women, entwining strands of female voices that were carried in female bodies, a phenomenon that seems to me cause for wonder and admiration, rather than suspicion of authorship.

At Kilcrea, the sky is darkening, and in my arms, my daughter is shivering and beginning to sing: 'Ba ba black she, How ya do the do?' I wrap my coat around us both as we stand where Eibhlín Dubh stood. I speak some lines from the *Caoineadh*, my voice springing back from the stone walls that once witnessed her voice too. When I say, 'Mo chara go daingean tú,' my daughter peers up at me, amused, then tilts her head sharply, mimicking the cadence of my words. I say it again, this phrase one might begin to translate as 'O, my steady companion.' I feel it so strongly here, her echo. This is our beginning.

—

Leaving Kilcrea, even my fingertips tingle electric. I wonder what I might learn of Eibhlín Dubh's days were I to veer away from the scholarship I have simply accepted thus far. I think again of all those blunt, brief sketches presenting this woman in the thin roles of aunt and wife, occluded by the shadows of men. How might she appear if drawn in the light of the women she knew instead?

By the time I step out of the car, I have devised a plan and chosen my tools. I may not be an academic, but I believe that I can sketch her years in my own way. I begin, of course, with a list. In addition to revisiting my previous reading, planning research trips to her homes, and tracing archival sources, I will return to a publication from 1892, *The Last Colonel of the Irish Brigade*. In two volumes of crisp, yellowed pages, an author who names herself as Mrs Morgan John O'Connell details a stash of family letters, found 'in old Maurice O'Connell's secretaire, brass-handled and many-drawered'. Maurice was Eibhlín Dubh's older brother, inheritor of the house they grew up in, and distributor of the family wealth. As one might expect, the letters between these brothers slant towards the concerns of men: military politics, trade arrangements, finances, and so on, but there are occasional references to the lives of women to be found there, too. I decide that I will return to these texts and commit an act of wilful erasure, whittling each document and letter until only the lives of women remain. In performing this oblique reading, I'll devote myself to luring female lives back from male texts. Such an experiment in reversal will reveal, I hope, the concealed lives of women, present, always, but coded in invisible ink.

In choosing a pair of women to draw Eibhlín Dubh with, I find that I don't need to search long. I am drawn towards the woman Mrs O'Connell refers to as '[Maurice and Daniel's] many-childed mother, with her weird gift of Irish improvisation, her practical shrewdness and good house-wifery', and when I discover that Eibhlín Dubh had a twin sister, I feel another path open itself to me. I begin to sketch her by the light of these two women, slowly braiding my research and daydream with the italics of Mrs O'Connell's book, and if a small voice in my head still asks 'Why?' it is quiet enough to ignore.

—

INSTRUCTIONS TO MAKE A MARIONETTE

1. Fold a page laundry-smooth.
2. Repeat. Repeat again, until the paper pleats resemble a pale accordion.
3. Sketch a female silhouette.
4. Use a sewing scissors to snip a woman of it.
5. In lifting her female outline from the cuttings, you are birthing her from the page. She is not alone. Observe how they all rise: hand in hand in hand.
6. Remember this lesson: in every page there are undrawn women, each waiting in her own particular silence.

—

éirigh suas anois,

rise up now,

—Eibhlín Dubh Ní Chonaill

When Eibhlín Dubh first floated in warm darkness, she was not alone. Even before her mother's fingertips discerned the bubble-twist of embryonic limbs, her twin was first to feel her stir against her.

—

An ocean before sunrise churns vast and vivid with countless individual ripples, each in its own momentum. In the half-light beyond the beach, a farmyard grows hectic, with horses nuzzling oats, eggs finding fists, and milk tumbling from udders, hiss by hot hiss. Inside the house, a girl strides into the parlour and kneels to yesterday's rubble-coals. Ash dances to her breath, and below, three embers begin to glow. From the kitchen, the smell of bread lifts, smooth white rolls speaking careful English for the family, brown loaves laughing in Irish for everyone else. Through each room lilts an excited murmuring, for today the woman of the house, Máire Ní Dhonnabháin Dhubh, is in labour.

This is not the first time her body had set upon the work of birthing; of the twenty-two children she will deliver in her lifetime, Máire will bury ten. A generous mistress, her sole thrift lies in her meticulous control over the household's eggs. Such is the contrast between her broad generosity and this particular tight-fistedness that she is affectionately nicknamed *Pianta Ubha* – 'Egg Pains' – a poignant choice, given the extent to which her ambitious body is bound to pregnancy. For decades, Máire's breasts are never far from milk, nor her womb from new life. Now, her body opens wide and her roars are joined by infant howlings – first one female voice. Then another. Twins. Girls. Máire falls back, thighs wet and shuddering. She names her newest daughters Eibhlín and Máire, but to all, they will be known as Nelly and Mary. Their mother does not rest long, for the running of Derrynane House is no small endeavour, and a profitable smuggling operation also falls under her supervision. Such 'trade' wasn't unusual then, but the scale of their practice did bring this family unusual wealth. Along with her husband, Dónal Mór, Máire conducts frequent departures of hides, salted fish, butter and wool, along with imports of tea and wine, sugar and brandy, tobacco, lush silks and velvets.

The two infant girls will be fostered to wet nurses until they are sturdy enough to rejoin their family at Derrynane House. When they return, it will be alongside a child of their foster family, an almost-sibling who will become a trusted servant-companion. The language the twins learn at the breasts of their foster mothers is Irish, but their home language is English, a linguistic dichotomy that is at the heart of this family. Mrs O'Connell writes,

> They spoke English, wore clothes of English fashion, and conformed more or less to English customs in everyday life; but they hankered in their hearts after the lost lands, the old tribal rights and privileges, and in moments of excitement used the Irish speech they had first learned.

By the time Nelly and Mary were born, the Penal Laws imposed by English colonisers had inflicted such brutality that the original social order had been, for the most part, demolished. These laws had been carefully devised to subjugate the native population and nullify any hazard that they might present to the Protestant Ascendancy, who now occupied their stolen lands. Irish Catholics were not to be educated, not allowed to hold possession of a horse worth more than £5, nor were they permitted to vote or bear arms. Unregistered priests were to be castrated; rewards were offered for a priest's decapitated head. There were, however, means whereby an ambitious matriarch could quietly contravene such a system. Derrynane Bay was remote and rarely visited by authorities, so here, Máire and her family could maintain a certain discretion. Enticements in the form of brandy and fine tobacco were sufficient to purchase silence.

In addition to managing home and trade, Máire was also a poet. Many of her surviving verses involve her addressing people at work in Derrynane. I translate one of the extant verses recorded by Mrs O'Connell as follows: 'Hurry now, ladies! Draw that yarn swiftly, for your spinning wheels are sturdy, and your bellies never hungry.' I find further fossils of her voice in the archives of University College Dublin, allowing me to imagine this woman as her daughters might have seen her, striding from courtyard to stable, her long, fair hair braided and neatly pinned up, dressed in the finest imported cloths, tailored to suit her taste of 'bright coloured silks opening over a satin petticoat, and fine lace caps and ruffles for dress, and the dimity and calamanco'. I set to translating one of these exchanges, in which Máire is boasting of her home: 'There's a low riverbank and a high riverbank, Shade from the heat and warmth from the cold, its face turns to the sun and its rear to the frost.' On hearing this sentimental outburst, a man nearby was said to counter –

There's a low riverbank and a high riverbank,
Its face to the frost and its rear to the sun,
Its middle squashed, and a rocky strand,
And that's all you have, Máire Ní Dhuibh.

There is such cleverness in this exchange of wit, in how deftly the rhythm of her initial boast is flipped through the retorts of servants, that one can almost imagine the hearty laughter that would follow it. When Máire pokes fun at a servant boy at breakfast: 'More than our own home and Ballinaboula, / I'd prefer an appetite as fine as my boy here', his retort again flips her own rhyme and metre, cleverly spinning a rejoinder:

Ah, but if you'd to wake early to hunt these lands,
and continue from here up to Ballinaboula,
then climb the steep hill to reap the sheaves,
and proceed to threshing in the barn,
then you, too, would be hungry, and as keen as me.

In the jocularity of such exchanges between the lady of the house and those in her employ, we sense something of the atmosphere that Máire Ní Dhuibh created around herself and her children. As a boss and as a mother, she prized a quickness of intellect and a certain audacity in conversation, which others responded to, remembered, and recounted.

Once weaned from the borrowed breasts of her foster-mother, little Nelly returned to Derrynane, laughing with her twin from stables to beach to forest. Overhead, branches hummed the whisper of the ancient oaks for which the place was named 'Derrynane', an Anglicisation of 'the great oak forest of Saint Fionán'. I want to hear the song that forest sang to Eibhlín Dubh as a girl, but I can't follow her while closed snugly within my own small rooms. I begin to consult maps. I circle dates on the calendar. I ready my car keys.

—

It's spring by the time I arrive at Derrynane to find that even in the depths of that forest, the aural tug of the tide turns the head like a magnet, letting me find my bearings as little Nelly did.

I'm alone on the beach where the sand stretches before me, countless fragments of shell and stone and quartz smashed into a new whole, a morning strand unmarked as yet by human presence. An empty page. Back then, it held new footprints every day, and the breeze held brief snatches of Portuguese, French, and Spanish. At low tide, the twins could scramble on foot to Abbey Island, just as I do.

Soft, the ground that met Nelly's skipping toes, Mrs O'Connell's long skirts, and now, my own heels. I turn, wanting to photograph the sight of my footprints in the sand I've longed to see, but in squinting at my phone screen I stumble over something. I catch myself and lift the obstacle: a blue-green rock, fist-sized, split by three intersecting bands of quartz. I choose to read it as an omen, a metaphor for intersecting existences, a sign that the three women I follow once walked here too. As I turn to the island, the stone grows warm by my skin.

Clambering up the island slope, I imagine the twins skipping through the squat juniper bushes, past wildflowers and the jagged greens of nettles. I feel certain that were Eibhlín Dubh to stand by my side now, she would immediately recognise this place, so little has changed, beyond the occasional rock tumbled by sea-gales, the ever-increasing number of gravestones, and the new cargo held below. In a corner of the ruined church, I find Máire's crypt:

She survived her husband 22 years
and was a model for wives and mothers
to admire and imitate.

Running my finger over the swirl and twist of these letters, I find myself saying her name, again and again. Am I summoning Eibhlín's mother or keening her?

'Máire,' I say, 'Máire.' I stand in silence a moment, and realise that I'm waiting for a response. No voice speaks back, but the wind rises to lash my hair against my cheek, sharp as a slap.

—

The path from the beach towards their home led the girls through the forest. Now, by the same path, I follow, through leaf-light that feels both present and antique. I move in a way I have never moved before: I amble slow, then slower still, in the hope that I might see something that could deepen my sense of Eibhlín Dubh's early days here. A little west of the house, I pause under gnarled oaks and beech trees, my heart fluttering like a bird. A tree has stumbled over, storm-blown. Embedded within its toppled tangle of root and soil are the remains of an old wall, and within that tangle is a door. It must have been swallowed by decades of the tree's growth, only to be exposed again by its fall. To scramble through, I would have to press my body close to that damp earth. I do. When I emerge, my knees are wet, and I feel different, though I can't say how. My right breast is already tingling. I walk on.

Ahead, I sense a lios before I see it, and though I fear it, I walk towards it. I know many scoff at the old tales that surround these ancient ringforts, but I refuse to shed my reverence for such dark and holy places. Beyond the house I grew up in, a lios interrupted the horizon. This was the heart that convulsed through all my inherited fears, dark and bleak and full of secrets, and though I stared at it often, I never dared approach it. All through my childhood I was told of the hazards that such places held: Others dwelled there, Others that our people had found to be very old and very shrewd, and those Others had been known to swipe girls like me. In school I was taught another way to translate the text of this landscape: ringforts were defensive enclosures that once sheltered farmsteads from wolves and thieves, we were told, and the stories attached to them were merely piseógs, or superstitious folklore. Mapped from above in my history textbook, a ringfort resembled an 'O', which reminded me of a cave mouth in a cliff, or some sort of portal. I did not want to know where such holes might go. The fabric of fear cloaked the image so thoroughly that I kept my distance. Today is different, though. Today, I feel that I am being led towards the lios by someone else. I can't resist it.

I walk closer, thinking that I see a shadow under the wall – or *in* the wall? Something is there. Something – dark – something – ajar. I find that what I had taken for the ringfort's perimeter wall is in fact a ring within a ring, and in between is a hollow chamber, like an inner corridor or a sequence of narrow rooms, still partially roofed with boulders. I have never seen anything like it. I poke my arm into the dark, feeling around the cold inner surfaces of the stones, patting blindly as though seeking a light switch in a darkened room. Then I give up and climb high. From above, I see that this fort is an elegant souterrain.

The word 'souterrain' holds its roots in French, drawing itself from *sous* (meaning 'under') and *terre* (meaning 'earth'). Underland. Underfoot. Underground. Under us. The sense of an ancient form constructed over a hidden architecture of depth – even this brings to mind the *Caoineadh*. I wonder what more I might find if I were to wait here a while. Although I am growing impatient to drive home to my children, I sit on the edge of the lios a moment and let my hands roam its surfaces, clothed in its rich green cape of grass and brambles. The position of this structure feels sheltered, almost cosy, in its nestling between the trees.

As I sit, a distant choreography of cloud and sunlight draws itself on my body. My fingertips stroll the stones. For what feels a long time, I sit and wait for this place to let something slip, to release some secret that might allow me to feel closer to the girl whose head once swivelled to the shout of two syllables through this forest: *Nel-ly, Nel-ly*. I think of the beginnings of growth she has already provoked in me. A tickle on my fist opens my eyes to find a small leaf bustling against it. Irritated, I shove it away and try to return to my reverie, but my gaze is already distracted, sprinting after its stem. From every tiny nook my fingers find the tenacious vines of wild strawberries. I see them in that moment, then, twin girls, one dark, one fair, their lips blushed with strawberry juice.

—

As a teenager, Nelly grew wild, so wild that at fourteen, her mother married her off to an old man recorded only as 'Mr Connor', who lived five hours away. Look: Nelly is tossing her comb into a chest with a small violence now, followed by a pair of nightdresses, embroidered stockings, and a locket. She slams the lid, then locks it. She embraces her twin sister tightly, but if they whisper, we are too far away to hear their words. When Nelly leaves Derrynane, a thousand sharp ripples glint their goodbyes.

—

I've read that a dowry in the form of sheep, horses, and cattle would often be driven ahead of a bride's carriage, so I send black cows trotting a narrow road and imagine Nelly pouting in the carriage that follows. A traditional 'hauling home' would demand that the bride's vehicle be heaved along the last stretch to a rowdy chorus of 'Óró, Sé Do Bheatha Abhaile', so as they approach their destination, watch their horses untethered as a merry crowd grabs the carriage instead. Nelly enters her marital home to whooping and applause, a fine wife everyone hopes will bring old O'Connor an heir. Within this house a harp is waiting. Once Nelly steps in, every one of its strings snaps. Tick. Tick. Tick. This oddity is read by all present as *A Very Bad Omen*, a fact communicated by the relay of a communal gasp that ripples through the crowd, and a tide of elbows poked in ribs. Unusual, to witness an omen in its birthing, when most omens can only be read in reverse. Once those strings split, every eye turns on Nelly.

Had no clear consequence followed the omen, this story would never have been told and retold until its echo grew strong enough to reach us. Within six months, however, her husband is dead, and his death lends doom to those strings, turning an ordinary (if strange) occurrence into a story worth repeating. Nelly must don her darkest frock and stand over his corpse to perform the text expected of her, before the same audience of eyes that witnessed the snapping of the strings. Some say she keened him, others that she sat back merrily cracking nuts at his wake, but either way, Nelly finds herself a widow at the age of fifteen. When she returns to Derrynane, she does not return pregnant.

Here: silence.

How I wish that someone had thought more women's words worthy of a place in that old secretaire. All the diaries and letters and ledgers I imagine in female handwriting, they must have existed once, until someone tidied them into a waste bin, tipping them neatly into oblivion. We are left with only the judgment of Mrs O'Connell (herself writing across both distance and decades) to gauge a sense of the aftermath of Nelly's marriage. Although Nelly 'neither entertained nor professed any special devotion for her husband, she regretted, on her return home, the loss of liberty and influence of the mistress of a household'.

I grow glum for this girl. I've become so accustomed to listening for echoes of her life in the life I know that she feels as real as any other unseen presence – as real as the disembodied voices on the radio, as real as the human chorus of the internet, as real as the roots stretching unseen under weeds, as real as the dog who howls beyond our hedge. She is real to me, as I follow her struggle from Derrynane to her failed marriage and back again; she is as real as I am.

I recognise how deeply different Eibhlín Dubh's life is from mine, and yet, I can't help myself in drawing connections between us. When I was a teenager, I, too, found myself staring down at a dead body, and I, too, found myself a failure. I was drawn to that moment by a room.

6. the dissection room

Is aisling trí néallaibh
do deineadh aréir dom

Last night, such clouded reveries
appeared to me ...

—Eibhlín Dubh Ní Chonaill

THE FIRST TIME I entered the room was in a dream.

In the dream, light was blazing through tall windows, and a number of indistinct forms were hovering at hip height, like mountain ranges under blankets of snow. The room felt recently emptied, as though a crowd of people unknown to me had just left; and in that brief moment of the room's emptiness I was suddenly present, a haunting.

When I woke, I pushed myself up on my elbows, shivering in disorientation and leftover awe; I shuddered as though hauling myself up from a river. The red digits of my stereo glared 08:52. It was a sunny

Saturday morning and I had overslept by three hours, which meant that I'd scuppered the first six of the fifteen study windows I'd plotted for my morning. Exam season was approaching. While my school friends were choosing between apprenticeships or courses in nursing or law, I had decided that there was one path above all others that would impose a steady structure on my future.

For a number of years, I had quietly observed our family dentist at work. He was an amiable man, calm and friendly, and it appeared to me that his working day involved a finite number of problems, each easily resolved by a series of well-defined manoeuvres. Even the sight of a broken tooth stretched from my own small, bloody palm had presented no difficulty to him. When I volunteered for work experience in his sunlit rooms, my instinct was confirmed: this was a good life. If I could secure high enough grades to study dentistry at university, it could be my life, too: safe, steady days, and a safe, steady paycheque.

My problem was that no one in the adult world agreed. The career-guidance teacher had spoken to my parents, frowning at the results of my aptitude tests and describing two options: teaching or teaching, either to children or teenagers. But the more adults who warned me that I was making a mistake in day-dreaming of dentistry, the more determined I became.

Beyond my smoking and drinking and the merry-go-round of dodgy boyfriends, I'd made dentistry the battleground of my teenage rebellion. I'd show them. I'd show all of them. I simply had to memorise a fixed volume of information and then release it on an exam paper. Easy.

I set to studying in every hour I could find: at home before the cows had even begun to crush their cud, during free periods at school, on the bus, and as I strode the small boreen home again. Even when I sneaked behind the school for a smoke, I fumbled for the list of French verbs in my pocket. I needed to learn by heart the conjugation I found most difficult, the Past Imperfect, in which the past was actively continuing. *Je désirais*: I was desiring, I was wanting, I was longing; the condition was never-ending. I turned every available moment of my life into an opportunity for rote learning. There were chemical equations to memorise, as well as verses of Yeats's poetry, definitions of cellular plasmolysis and crenation, an entire essay on the Ottoman Empire between 1453 and 1571. There was so much I needed to do. I needed to memorise the laws of genetics, how the processes of transcription and translation differ in DNA reproduction. I needed to practise quadratic equations. I needed to solve for x and for y. I couldn't afford to waste any time, but now, I was waking far behind schedule, my body still thrumming with exhilaration at my dreamed vision.

When I threw open the door to my parents' bedroom I found them chewing buttered toast and smiling in sunlight, as radio headlines hummed in the background. I told them how I'd dreamt a church-kind-of-place and that it felt so real, that I knew this must be an omen that everything was going to be OK, that I could see it all so clearly now. My dad was gathering their cups. 'You need more sleep,' he smiled. By this point, the dynamic of our conversations on my future was well established. 'If you chose Arts you could study four different subjects,' my mother would say, 'you love history, you could do that, and English, if you wanted to, and philosophy, and anything else you wanted!' They made an Arts degree sound like Christmas, but I felt certain that it would lead to no job, no safety, and no control. I knew they were worried about me: that I was studying instead of sleeping, that I wasn't eating, that I was thin and tense and smoking too much. I knew they thought that if I chose a path that demanded less of me, that I would be happier; I also knew that they were wrong. I'd be seventeen soon. I had a plan. I could make it happen.

In the shower, I focused on the diagram of the small intestine I'd taped to the outside of the glass and repeated the labels to myself until they sounded like prayer: *epithelial cells, microvilli, lymphatic lacteal, lumen.* I closed my eyes and repeated them as the image reconstructed itself in my mind: *lumen, lumen, lumen.* Scald-water rose from my arms in a haze, dissipating from skin to air.

———

The second time I entered the room, a corpse was waiting.

That morning, I'd opened my eyes in a strange bedroom to the sound of a river. I'd won a small scholarship that allowed me a bedroom in a shared campus flat, and on my first night, and every night afterwards, I slept with my window open, letting the sound of the Lee soothe me to sleep. I dressed, pinned up my hair, drank a glass of milk, smoked four cigarettes, triple-checked my bag, slid foam headphones over my ears, and pressed play on my walkman. The Pixies roared in my ears as I marched up the hill, checking my campus map twice as I went.

In the registration queue for first-year pre-medical students, the others spoke with the honeyed vowels of private schools. I read them hungrily, my class-mates: their tans, their gestures, and the slant of their collars. We each carried brand-new dissection pouches purchased in the university shop along with a heap of textbooks. When I overheard some jokes about inherited lab coats, I translated the underlying text to myself. My own was factory-new and heavily starched, an abrasive skin I'd buttoned myself into and now couldn't shrug off. As I sat in the lecture theatre, my neck itched wildly, but I held my spine tight, and restrained myself from scratching it.

A lecturer strode in and the room quietened. The technician slid a video into the VCR. The TV flickered, then resolved into an image of a naked body. Dead, I thought. *Dead?* Dead. A friendly voice began to narrate proceedings:

> *THORAX. Observe the scalpel's neat incision, beginning between the clavicles, down the sternum, to the umbilical. The edges of the incision are held firmly. A smaller scalpel is preferable at this point, to explore beyond superficial layers of fat and fascia. Once the skin is removed, observe the ribs and their intercostal musculature. Clear the pectoral muscles from the rib cage with care. A handsaw is –*

As the video stuttered and, finally, failed, the technician gave the machine a weary thump. When nothing stirred, the lecturer led us into the lab, handing each of us a pair of latex gloves as we entered. With a jolt, I found myself standing in the landscape I'd dreamt months before. The same high ceiling, the same blazing windows: it was all precisely, eerily the same. Even those weird mountainscapes – about ten of them – were the same, but this time, rather than hovering, each one was supported by the legs of a trolley and covered by a sheet. Unlike my sleeping self, I could guess what lay below. How had my dream revealed this room to me, in all its vividness? The shock of the recognition was such that it forced a bodily response: a cold sweat began to form on my scalp and my gloves felt too tight suddenly. For one long, suspended moment, I was stilled in bewilderment. Then a tall girl jostled past, and my legs moved me to follow her.

There were six of us at the table, and all of us were silent. When I reached into the pocket of my lab coat to mimic their readiness, a scalpel slid through the pouch and sheared the tip of my finger. (Tick.) I hurried to the bathroom, tugged off my glove, sucked the blood from the wound, then wrapped it in wadded tissue and slid a new glove over it, hoping that no one would laugh at my weirdly padded hand. I stared at myself in the mirror. Who slices themselves open in a dissection room? Only me, only me.

When I returned, the others were nodding at each other like old ladies around a fresh pot of tea, 'You first.' 'No, please, after you,' etc., etc. The lecturer, I gathered, had delivered the instructions in my absence; now it was time to commence the dissection.

Eventually, one lavishly freckled boy inhaled, chose a scalpel, and folded the white sheet from the cadaver's throat to its waist. We all leaned over the cold expanse of human skin.

I had always imagined that the body I dissected would look much like my own naked body, but this was a very elderly person; also dead; also embalmed. Above a round little tummy, small breasts sagged softly, speckled with liver spots. There was a smell, of course there was, not the smell I had imagined, but a recognisably bodily smell nonetheless, simultaneously fleshy and chemical in nature, something like a dog on a hot day, if someone tripped and sloshed a bucketful of disinfectant mop liquid over it. The boy held the blade over the old woman's body for one trembling moment. Then he brought it down. He cut her. The room was gripped by silence as all the other students at all the other trollies bent over bodies too, all our mouths ajar, enchanted. And then, as though by silent agreement, we began to cut. I watched skin lifted from the old woman's ribcage in two drab flaps, like the wings of a moth. Hand after hand pressed scalpel to skin, trimming at fat and prodding muscle. Why had she chosen this, I wondered – what might drive a person to inflict such a brutal ending on their own body? I tried to join in, poking ineffectually at flesh that seemed uncannily like tinned tuna, grey and layered, but my mind was still turning over the weirdness of standing in the room I had dreamt.

For the next few weeks I spent my evenings thumbing through textbooks to prepare for dissection classes, memorising anatomical nomenclature. I developed a gentle camaraderie with my classmates, who were given to a shared vocabulary of jokey gestures I didn't fully understand – a sudden poke in the ribs, say, while laughing: 'Hah! You jumped!' The game was to feign composure against the instinct of the body. I always failed; I just didn't get it. Only months earlier, I'd been smoking behind our school when an ex-boyfriend sneaked up and pressed the cold blade of a flick-knife against the back of my school jumper. That was a joke, too. Here, there were different knives and different jokes, but my laugh sounded false as ever. One Monday, a girl told me that she'd been skiing for the weekend. 'Super!' I bleated, an alien word I uttered too often that year, and never since. I grinned so much in that room that whenever I lay in my narrow bed, listening to the night-river humming its inherited song, my cheeks ached.

Day by day, the cadaver changed. Every slice of mangled viscera, muscle, and cartilage we removed was to be tossed into a blue plastic bucket – a kind of tidying into a kind of bin – where they lay like jigsaw pieces, or fragments of a fallen vessel. We had been told that after the dissection was complete, all the buckets of cuttings, along with the hollowed shell of bone and skin, would be neatly coffined and driven to a crematorium or a graveyard. There, a family would gather to say beautiful words, honouring the person who had inexplicably given their body to us.

I never saw anyone treat a cadaver with anything other than whispered respect and a gentle blading, but in the pub we threw back shots of Sambuca and roared together at the same implausibly gory punch-lines: '... and then just after last call, the guy stood at the top of the line at the urinal and just dropped the corpse's cock in, and as it poured by each of the other guys, they all puked into the water'. While we laughed, the room was empty. The room was dark. The lights were all switched off.

As the semester progressed, I was rarely in the dissection room. The more friends I made, the more I drank; the more I drank, the more I smoked; the more I smoked, the less I ate. I only felt like myself when I saw want in a stranger's eyes; I remembered when I had wanted something too. I gave myself away to that desire and it felt good to be carried elsewhere in the cold surge of it. On hungover afternoons, I still dragged myself to the library, building ramparts of volumes on physiology and dissection around my desk, stuffing a ring-binder full of photocopied diagrams and borrowed lecture notes I never read. I suppose I was at least pretending to myself that I would attend the next session, but I always happened to find myself out on the tear the night before anatomy lab, and often, the following morning, I just didn't turn up. I only half know where I was instead: asleep with a cheek on a toilet seat, or opening an eye to the smell of a stranger's flatmate frying rashers, or drooling on a pillow that wasn't mine. I wasn't where I was supposed to be. I wasn't in the room when I panic-scrubbed my vomit from my flatmate's favourite (borrowed) dress. I wasn't in the room on the many mornings when I collected the morning-after pill from yawning chemists. I wasn't in the room when I wept in the chapel of a cloistered order of nuns. I wasn't in the room when I dozed in A&E, my head nodding over red bandages, with shards of a pint glass embedded in my fist. I wasn't in the room the morning after I tried to give my body to the river. I wasn't in the room. I had left.

I had left, and yet every now and then, I dragged myself back to the anatomy lab. I remember entering the room uncharacteristically early one morning with a whiskey hangover and dirty hair. I stood by the sheeted cadaver and stared at raindrops bevelling the window-glass, distorting the view, making the city rooftops seem malleable. Beyond, clouds clotted, heavy and silver grey, preparing to drop rain, or dropping it already. I leaned my weary body against the trolley, hoping someone might show up who knew what they were doing. I would like to say that this was a moment of profound connection with the human who had donated her body for the purposes of my learning, or that I promised her I'd find a way to make up for my abandonment, but that would be a lie. I ignored the person under the sheet. All I could think about was how badly I was gasping for a smoke. Bored, I bit my fingernails, tearing sharp fragments away with my teeth, swallowing, biting again. Next, I nipped the cuticle skin by the lunulae, peeling it away in thin shreds, biting and swallowing until every finger bled. When I imagined all those bits of finger flesh and molecules of blood churning in my stomach, I began to feel woozy again.

The others filed in – clever, glossy-haired, thoughtful – and although they tried to make small talk with me, I just smiled queasily, sweating in shame. I had come in search of a secure life, but there was no safety here, there was no control. I should never have come. I was failing every subject. I was a mess.

The sheet rolled back.

So much had changed since my last visit. The ribcage was gone, as were the lungs. The calvarium had been sawn off, and the skull lay open, but the brain was absent. An arm had been neatly carved to display the layers of vessels within. The face was ... ajar. I don't remember the eyes, either because I couldn't bring myself to look or because I stared at them too long. What remained was a sharply grey architecture that was difficult to read as human, and yet it seemed more human than I felt. I couldn't open my kit. I stood and watched instead, as a pair of scissors forced its way through the pericardial sac, its glint and twist quick as a key in the keyhole of an antique chest. Inside, I knew, was the heart.

Next, a scalpel sliced the blood vessels away, a process nothing like the delicate ritual I had imagined, more like taking a steak knife to a garden hose. The heart was grey, but it seemed to shine, somehow. Scooped up, it was passed from hand to hand to hand. I held it gently, and it really did shine, as morning light illuminated a line of staples that protruded from the muscle. The lab technician pointed as he hurried past: 'Ah – as we discussed – cardiac surgery.' It seemed peculiar that a heart could be repaired so clumsily and continue to carry a body through its days. And yet here it was: a heart stitched and stapled; a heart twice removed and held in the hands of others.

—

The third time I entered the room I entered in darkness.

It was an evening in late November, and I wore my infant son strapped to me in a sling, his hot belly tucked close, fontanelle throbbing under my chin. On a whim, I'd decided to attend a book launch on campus, telling myself it might be interesting to revisit the building ten years later. After that disastrous first year, I had switched to an Arts degree and studied psychology and English, before eventually becoming a teacher. I found that I loved spending my days in the company of thirty-five children, teaching them to read and paint and count. I didn't regret my year studying dentistry, but sometimes, when my classroom filled with a certain slant of sunlight, I was struck again by the puzzling intersection of my dream and the dissection room. I had never forgotten that room; I wondered whether it had forgotten me.

After the launch speeches, after I'd joined in with the applause and dutifully purchased the book, I hefted my sling straps high and stole away from lukewarm chat, wine and cheese-sticks. It had always been bright when I studied here, but even in the dark I knew my way back to the dissection room. Outside, I hesitated, hand hovering over the doorknob. There would be no cadavers inside, I knew, for the intervening decade had seen an elaborate new centre constructed nearby, the Facility for Learning Anatomy, Morphology, and Embryology, more commonly known by its acronym: the FLAME Lab. The door was stiff when I tried the knob, but it yielded to my shoulder-bone. I dithered on the threshold, scared of the dark, but more scared of flicking the switch in case the light might draw a security guard to investigate. I stepped into the darkness. The room was empty.

I made my way to the spot I'd always occupied among the cadavers. Pressing my brow to the window, I felt the sill, cool under my palm. Some dust had gentled itself to rest there, with the ordinary beauty of minuscule things, and I imagined its many components: an atom of lead scraped from an ancient pencil, the silver fleck of some long-ago cigarette, specklets of dandruff, old, old ash, a fragment of grit picked from a fingernail, and the imperceptibly tiny remnants of bodies dissected here. I ran my finger along the sill, touched the smudge to my tongue, and swallowed.

A thud from the yard beyond set my heart juddering, and a new sensation fidgeted and grew: the sense that if I stayed, something in this room might shift to reveal something vast, something I hadn't yet understood. There was so much here that I had already struggled to comprehend, so I whispered my farewell and turned away instead, telling myself that I'd never come back to this room again. The baby turned in his sleep and uncurled his clammy fist, fingers starfishing against my collarbone. When my hand met the door-knob, the beginnings of milk tingled, and my nipple began to itch. I resisted the desire to scratch it.

—

The fourth time I entered the room I was a thief.

I'd seen on Facebook that the building was tempo-rarily vacant in preparation for extensive renovations, and the faculty had given permission for an art exhi-bition. I knew before I closed that tab that I would soon stand in the room again.

I was determined to make some sort of sense out of my attraction to this place and its intersection with my dream. In the car park, I tapped my phone through a phenomenon known as *déjà revé*: a title, if not an explanation, for the experience of dreaming something and then living it in reality. What had happened to me was called a precognitive dream: a premonitory vision, or an omen, experienced in sleep, but the websites offered no convincing explanation, and enough of them bore images of crystal balls and scantily clad cartoon fairies to irritate me.

If my dream had literally come true, then why had I fucked it all up? The whole plot seemed so far-fetched that were a novelist to implant such a moment in a book, I would roll my eyes. And yet, I thought, if I was a fictional character who had seen her dream come true and then cartwheeled her way to spectacular failure, what would she do now? She wouldn't sit in a car poking her phone around hippy-dippy websites. No. She'd go in.

The door had been wedged open by a bockety chair on which was sellotaped a hand-scrawled sign: ART THIS WAY. Upstairs, daylight showed elements of the room that had escaped me on my previous visit. The cold elevator that drew cadavers up from the basement. The sinks still stained with years of con-centric metallic rings. I began to worry that unless I paid attention to the exhibition, I would be asked to leave, so I strolled around projections and canvases while surreptitiously studying the changes that had occurred at their peripheries. The delicate vine of ivy that had penetrated the window frame. The cobweb under a tap. The cracks writing their own slow histo-ries through the plaster. The thick dust underlining each tile.

Behind me, a pair of students clicked a selfie. One rolled a Rizla between fingertips of splintered blue nail polish, licked it and pressed. When she smiled and said, 'Back in a sec,' I nodded. As soon as the door rapped behind them, I took the back stairs in three leaps to the mezzanine, where I had never been, and into the office of the anatomy technician. The drawers of various storage units were open, their papers scattered all over the floor. A thin grime cloaked the surfaces. I figured I might have five minutes before the others returned from their smoke. What to do? I surprised myself by wrenching open a side door and racing up an older, narrower stairway.

The attic was cold with a hidden-room stench of damp and stone, and brickwork clothed in the filthy silk of ancient cobwebs. I was standing exactly above the dissection room. Through this shadowy upper room, something of each of those people might have risen – call it a soul – lifting though rafter and slate, as steam dissipates from skin to air. For a moment, I stood still, thinking of the generations of bats and mice who lived whole lives here while humans dismantled human bodies below. What could I do that might force some reasonable ending to this story? I closed my eyes until I grew lightheaded. Then I chose something to steal.

When I got home, I didn't know what to do with my theft. The brick was encrusted with mortar and grimy with old, old dust. It was ugly and weird, and I couldn't explain why I had stolen it. I was embarrassed. First, I hid it from myself under a chair in the sitting room. Then, I leaned it behind a plant. I didn't want to be able to see the brick – it had been another stupid mistake to steal it – but I couldn't stop thinking about it. I couldn't bring myself to keep it in the house, but I couldn't return it either. This is how the brick came to live in the grass, tucked between stones I'd hauled back from beach trips and ruined demesne walls. There it remains, host to lichen, brief shelter to wild bees and butterflies, slid over by snails.

—

I knew it was simply a matter of time before I'd return to the room. I had taken and taken so much, I longed to find some way to balance the equation. One morning, I rang a number. The next, forms arrived. My scrawled signature was all that was needed to pledge my body to the dissection room. A gesture into the distance, it felt easy as pressing my car key from afar; I simply slid the envelope into the post-box and felt a door unlock itself for me.

If it was a relief to imagine that my body would someday become one of the hundred cadavers wheeled into the rooms of five Irish medical schools every year, and it also made my dream feel more prophetic than ever. These institutions are united in their positions on the emotional impulses that drive such donations. NUIG's website states: 'Body donation is a most generous and charitable gesture and it is with deep gratitude that we at Anatomy, NUI Galway, accept bequests of this manner, for they help us train the future generation of medical doctors and medical scientists.' The Royal College of Surgeons refers to how the 'unique and priceless gift of the human body provides a source of knowledge that is the foundation of medical education and research'. Trinity College: 'Our department is utterly dependent on the generosity of spirit of those who donate their bodies to Medical Science.' UCC: 'The generous act of body donation is vital to the study of human anatomy.' UCD: 'Through the selfless act of donating your body to medical education, one can make a huge impact upon the life and wellbeing of others for generations to come ... The School is eternally indebted to the many individuals who chose to donate their bodies to clinical education and their families who support this generous gift.'

I'm not sure if the act of donating one's corpse to an anatomy department can be fully explained by the simplicity of generosity or selflessness; I suspect that such a gesture holds more complexity than these institutions might imagine. It might also be construed, for example, as a failed attempt to exert some control over the body's fate after death, or as a convenient way to pay burial costs. Historically, next of kin were permitted to donate the corpse of another in exchange for such costs. Medical schools still compensate a donor's family for eventual burial or cremation costs, a fact that is a reassurance to me – at least my family won't have to concern themselves with such bills. The poetics of the gesture please me too, allowing me to orchestrate a moment of my future in which my body will echo a moment from my past. Despite my failure as a student of anatomy, the experience of watching a human body disassembled was one of the most profound of my life. I am still moved by the remembered sensation of holding another person's heart in my hands. One morning, when I am dead, a stranger will lift my own heart in their hands. Even if they giggle or play pranks on my body, their laughter will be a form of afterlife I am happy to give myself to.

I wanted to leave a message for the strangers who would be the last to touch me. In choosing white ink for my tattoo, I thought of the milk bank. I thought of the *Caoineadh* emerging from a sequence of pale throats. I thought of all the absent texts composed by women, those works of literature never transcribed or translated. I thought of Hélène Cixous: 'there is always within her at least a little of that good mother's milk. She writes in white ink.' I knew then that I must choose the words of Eibhlín Dubh. The fragment I chose occurs when she wakes suddenly from a dream in which a prophetic vision is revealed to her, 'Is aisling trí néallaibh', which I translate as 'such clouded reveries'.

When the tattooist's needle approached, I pinched my eyelids closed and let the pain carry me to the room for the fifth time. As her words were etched into my skin, letter by pale letter, I saw those old windows once more, cathedral-elegant, and glazed in blazing sunlight.

7. cold lips to cold lips

Níor throm suan dom

No slumber hampered me

—Eibhlín Dubh Ní Chonaill

I NEVER GREW OUT of the habit of reading by fingertip. Now, whenever I search archives for references to Eibhlín Dubh, the line of my scalpel-scar mirrors the pale space between lines of text. My skin remembers that blade well, but it is rare that these antique papers remember her name. I try to find her. I try and try and fail and fail. Eventually I return to Mrs O'Connell's enviable access to the letters of her brothers. Perhaps the compulsion to lay a woman's life before me and slowly explore each layer started in the dissection room; so many of our most steadfast patterns are begun in those years between childhood and adulthood.

—

Nelly was still a teenager when she returned to Derry-nane. I calculate that the twins would only share three further years of each other's company before being separated by another marriage. Whereas Nelly was now a dark-haired, teenaged widow, her twin sister Mary is described by Mrs O'Connell as 'the flower of the flock, blue-eyed and golden-haired'. Whenever a ship ran aground, the family proved generous hosts to those in need. I imagine the twins spying on the crews' comings and goings, lifting skirts from their ankles as they dodged puddles. Soon, the sight of splinters on the tide brought a lover to their strand.

While waiting to arrange passage home, an English aristocrat named Herbert Baldwin fell in love with Mary. He made up his mind quickly: he would marry this Irish girl and bring her back to England: *happy ever after*. How taken aback he must have been when his proposal was rejected by her parents. Máire believed that if her golden Mary were to marry an aristocrat, she would always appear a bumpkin by comparison. She would have preferred her daughter be considered noble in a simple marriage, than simple in a noble marriage. No matter how Herbert implored her to re-consider, Máire shook her head. Eventually he left, vowing to secure written assurances from his family for Mary's hand. Máire smiled. Máire began to plan a marriage.

In lieu of Mary's sweetheart, Máire selected another Baldwin from a prosperous family of English descent, based in Clohina, County Cork. Poor Mary – although he was rich, Mrs O'Connell writes that this man 'by no means struck her fancy, as he was not young, and was a tall, gaunt, long-limbed personage'. In his youth, James Baldwin had been disowned for a time following his conversion to Catholicism – a perplexingly strange decision in Penal times. In 1762, three years after Nelly's return to Derrynane as a widow, Mary set to packing her own trousseau. How often did her gaze read the horizon in search of a ship? How long did hope pulse within her? When she left Derrynane it was with a generous dowry of 120 black cattle, an unrecorded sum of cash, ponies, a riding mare of her own, and the foster-sister she had known since infancy, Cathy Sullivan. At the meal following the wedding, many notes of congratulations were received. Among them was a letter from England, a letter that held a formal invitation for Mary to become Herbert's wife. Too late, too late. Mary was already Mrs James Baldwin. *The End.*

—

All her life, Mary had been a 'good girl'. Now she proceeded to excel at the parameters of success that had been sketched for a woman in her position. Having accepted her mother's choice of husband and brought a fine dowry to the household, her first decade at Clohina saw her birth six children. Her family must have been pleased with such achievements. However, Mary did not forget what might have been – holding her third infant, she named him Herbert.

Mrs O'Connell recounts how 'when even the best of husbands are apt to be a little tiresome, sometimes, she could always put down her spouse by observing "But for you, Mr Baldwin, I might have been Countess of Powis,"' a retort that brings to mind the wit of her mother.

Máire, meanwhile, must have felt sorry for the little widow moping around Derrynane strand, because it wasn't long before Nelly was given permission to visit her twin.

—

I describe these lives as though they were easily conjured, but that is not true. I mulled over these early years of Eibhlín Dubh's for months. Whenever there wasn't space for both of us in my days, I chose her needs over mine, skipping meals and showers and sleep – an impulse that came easily, as I was accustomed to shunning my own desires to serve the needs of others. I turned every available moment of my life towards learning more of hers. I grew thin. Despite the dark circles that swelled under my eyes, despite my unclean hair and echoing stomach, I was comforted by the thought that this labour might somehow prove worthwhile. I just wasn't sure how.

Milk was inextricable from my labours: my body responded to my daughter's hunger with a rush of milk, and then my mind responded to the milk by rushing back to the scattered jigsaw of Eibhlín Dubh's days. Whenever I felt milk move along my inner paths of ducts and lobules, I thought of udders swaying along a dirt boreen towards a harp in the distance, its strings taut, still. In her sleep, my daughter gulped.

—

From Clohina, the twins decided to take a jaunt to the town. There, Nelly's gaze dawdled towards the market. Impossibly handsome and extravagantly attired, Art Ó Laoghaire did not merely walk through her line of vision. He swaggered. As her eye followed him, a verse was being composed by her future self, the first verse of a poem Nelly couldn't have imagined yet, a text that would carry her to this stranger's death, a text that would outlive all of them. This is the moment that opens the *Caoineadh* –

> The day I first saw you
> by the market's thatched roof,
> how my eye took a shine to you,
> how my heart took delight in you,
> I fled my companions with you,
> to soar far from home with you.

These lines occur simultaneously in two landscapes, both in a busy streetscape, and within a female body. The poet portrays herself as the active party – it is she who sees Art, it is she who feels the physical twist of desire and of love, and it is she who chooses to flee with him.

Like Nelly's, Art's family had found a way to thrive quietly under the vicious regime of the Penal Laws, his father having secured employment with a prosperous family of landlords. As land agent to the Minhears, he worked as an intermediary, collecting rent from local farmers and delivering it to his bosses. This role allowed him to lease a farm at Raleigh, a short ride from Macroom. Although it may sound English, in this case *Raleigh* is an Anglicisation of

Ráth Luíoch: the ringfort of Luíoch. For an ambitious man like Art – one of a younger generation of what had once been a noble family of the Gaelic gentry – the reality of the Penal Laws meant that he was barred not only from accessing education, but also from behaving publicly like the gentleman he felt himself to be. Once he came of age, his father set aside sufficient funds to pay Art's passage to Austria by sea and by land, as well as purchasing a commission for him in the Austro-Hungarian army, loyal to Empress Maria Theresa. Within his regiment, the Hungarian Hussars, Art swiftly rose to the rank of captain, making such a name for himself that the Empress gifted him his own horse, as well as a decorative bronze eagle and two large ornamental statues of soldiers. These sculptures followed Art home, moving across Europe by covered wagon, by sea, and by road. Eventually they would be fixed to the courtyard walls of Raleigh House, gifts from the mother of a little girl who would grow up to be a French queen, and who would later kneel at a guillotine.

Art was fearless, or foolhardy, or both. Whenever he returned home on leave, he made a spectacle of himself, flaunting a sword in public, say, or running on top of a barrel as it rolled down Main Street. In doing so, he was also making a spectacle of the laws designed to crush him. To a teenager accustomed to watching men behave with fearful deference, his strut must have seemed hopelessly glamorous. Nelly's eye clung to his body as it moved. Nelly found herself desiring an introduction. Nelly found herself desiring.

—

Of all that I desired in my own small life, the discovery of another woman's days had become what I wanted more than anything else. More, even, than sleep. In pursuing this struggle, my principal nemesis was myself. I was weary. No, I was exhausted, and yet, my determination outweighed my body's desires. No matter how inconsequential they might have appeared to a bystander, any new detail I came across felt precious to me. I hoarded every scanty fact and carried them through my own days, untethering my imagination as I did my chores, or bathed my children, or sat in traffic. I hoovered and scrubbed and read stories and wrestled duvets into coverlets, and all the while, inside me, she was beginning to feel more and more real.

Whenever I found myself too tired to continue, I felt I was failing Eibhlín Dubh. I grew angry with myself. In desperation, I took to drinking coffee late, tipping its hot ink into my mouth with a tequila-flinch. I kept my phone by my bed as everyone else slept, tapping notes and images and new lists onto my screen. In that darkness, I was thinking about desire and power. I was seeing Mary's wedding ring, Nelly's grin, or Art's shadow as it slid over the walls I knew in Macroom. Every night, I was brawling against my body until it fought back, dropping my eyelids mid-sentence, releasing my fingers so that my phone went crashing to the floor. Every night I repeated the ritual, lying awake as long as my body would let me, listening carefully in case she might knock. There was a knocking – I could hear it, dim and weary – but it rose from within my own chest.

—

That this new couple spent time smiling in each other's company, we may safely assume. Perhaps we may also assume that there may have been the occasional furtive touch or kiss, but we cannot know how such moments were arranged, monitored, or thwarted. I wonder whether Mary was dragged along too – poor Mary, vigilant or bored in her role as chaperone; poor Mary, pregnant again and tired, longing to be at home.

It takes some time to pinpoint the location of Clohina House. I squint at old maps, determined to match the jagged boundaries of old roads and fields to contemporary satellite images. The landscape looks so different when I arrive that I grow confused, driving slow loops around the area I suspect she knew. Eventually, I hop out and stand on the lip of a boreen, trying to peer through a tangle of brambles, but I can't see beyond it. I grow impatient, feeling the inner itch that tells me that I'm running out of time, that my daughter will soon be calling for milk at home. On a whim, then, I ask Mary herself to show me to her home. I tell myself that such an oblique approach is in keeping with the strangeness of my mission, and yet, I cringe at the sound of my voice. A sceptic might call it coincidence that a car soon slows by my side, and that inside is a farmer who asks if I'm lost. He knows the Baldwins' old place, he says, leading me to the wet meadow where Mary's rooms once stood. 'See?' he says. 'Nothing.' He walks away, leaving me perched on a six-bar gate, peering at the empty air where a poem of beautiful rooms once stood, each stanza holding its own careful litany: the parasols, portraits, and books, the blue vases and embroidered blankets, the drapes and the sideboards, the letters, the combs, and the coats, the spoons and looking-glasses and scrubbing cloths, the coal buckets and diaries and piss-pots. Now: nothing. Another grand deletion, this. Another ordinary obliteration of a woman's life. The farmer is right, I am looking at nothing. I am also looking at everything.

—

There are many moments in Nelly's life that I won't let myself sketch in the absence of evidence, because to do so would feel like trespass, or theft. Whenever I can't bring myself to imagine the gap where a jigsaw piece should be, I look instead towards its periphery. Rather than imagining the intimacies of Nelly and Art's courtship, I find myself thinking of the imperceptible beat in which a word exists, between the articulation and the hearing. I sketch the couple apart rather than together. First, the urge, the pulse, the need. Then the smile, the mischief, the little desire in its little flickering. Next, the paper, the quill's pause, the hover, the liquid drop: blot, blot. The human effort to articulate a want and a love. The scratch of nib to paper, the liquid birth and loop of the letters, each connected to the next, word following word, and all the small spaces that exist between them. The paper sealed and sent on its way. The strange silence between a letter's departure but before its delivery, the curious time after words have been imagined and imprinted on paper, but before they are read. The letter as a kinetic object of desire, in motion from one body to another. These spaces between Nelly and Art are all that I let myself see, how after a letter had left, one might linger at a window, imagining it held in the grip of a lover, and one's own words moving quietly over another's lips.

—

Art is galloping, now.

His horse's sides are heaving and frothing. He draws the reins to a trot, smears sweat from brow to glove, then shades his eyes. The ocean, dazzling, and beyond, Derrynane. Nearly there.

Now, the door. Now, the rap of knuckle-bones.

Now, the swish-hiss of skirts, the silver song of keys: Máire.

For one swaying moment, she is on one side of a portal and Art is on the other, his fist in mid-air, weighing a second knock, while her hand approaches the door handle.

The door opens.

Their eyes meet. Máire is as quick in her assessment of trouble as he is in his.

Both smile.

Art is welcomed with the same hospitality extended to any young man finding himself far from home. When he clears his throat, his palms are open and bright, but as soon as he says Nelly's name, the heads of both parents shake. Art is a threat, and a noisy one at that; even the temporary presence of such a character could mean trouble. Despite their dismissal, Art grins. He has no cause to feel discouraged. He knows their daughter well.

—

When I brew myself a cup of tea something always interrupts me, and my tea grows slowly cold while I buzz about more chores, with a baby on one shoulder and a dish-towel on the other. I have made my peace with drinking repeatedly abandoned and re-microwaved tea.

Once the baby sleeps, I sit and blow again on that old steam, and Eibhlín Dubh tiptoes in to join me in my daydreams. I am never alone.

Today, I hold my cup and imagine her belongings into being. I give her a large, sturdy chest with a clasp of polished brass. Within, the ordinary treasures of a life: a locket, a favourite cup wrapped in a blanket, a shell, a quill, a diary, nightdresses and gowns, a looking-glass, a heavy winter cloak, table linens, a necklace, and a clutch of letters neatly ribboned together. I will never touch the belongings I conjure for her, and yet, each one feels right to me as I imagine lifting them to the light and then placing them back in her chest, one by one. Our possessions are as fleeting as our days; how quickly it all vanishes. Upstairs, the baby is already stirring from sleep – I hear a cry and I am soon running up the stairs again. Somewhere behind me, steam lifts and disappears.

———

To order a new gown is to pinch fabric between thumb and fingertip, and to choose a form into which it will be bound by seams of neat stitches. Thread is touched to a tongue. The needle is pushed through cloth, again and again and again, each stitch and scissor snip following a distinct pattern. The thread is bitten, the knot tied, the body buttoned into the garment, the flowers severed and bound. There are eyes on either side of the aisle. They observe the woman's slow arrival. They smile.

—

It was late 1767 when this couple married. December. A shiver-bright day. Art was twenty-one, and Nelly twenty-four. They pressed cold lips to cold lips and watched their names written side by side, a text that could not be undone. I set sunlight glinting through the windows where they swore to be true to each other until death. Turning together, they faced the door that led to the rest of their lives. The aisle returned the sound of their footfall as they left: *for-ev-er, for-ev-er.* Their marriage was to last six years.

No letter exists that voices the response of any of the family's women to this elopement, but her brothers' reaction survives. On 26 May 1768, six months after the ceremony, Maurice received a letter from his brother Daniel in France: 'I am sorry to learn that our sister Nelly has taken a step contrary to the will of her parents, but love will not know nor hear reason.'

In eschewing her dowry and Derrynane, she left part of herself behind too. Nelly was gone. Unlike Mrs Baldwin of Clohina, this twin would never be known as Mrs O'Leary. In choosing her own husband, she would choose her own name. Her surname remained Ní Chonaill, while 'Dubh' moved in the antique way from the mother's name to the daughter's, from Máire Ní Dhonnabháin Dhubh – Máire of the Dark Donovans – to Eibhlín Dubh Ní Chonaill. The more I sit with even the most cursory details of this woman's existence, the more is revealed. Here, a name is never simply a name. The 'Dubh' in Eibhlín Dubh – the darkness in her – comes from her mother.

I wonder what darkness I may leave embedded in my daughter.

8. oubliette

Mo ghrá is mo rún tú!
'S mo ghrá mo cholúr geal!

O my love and my dear!
O my love and my bright dove!

—Eibhlín Dubh Ní Chonaill

I HAD ALWAYS HOPED to name a daughter for the ocean, but lying under the long fluorescent bulbs outside the birthing room, I changed my mind. On impulse, I chose a name that means *Light*; I don't remember why. Now, every time I throw open the curtains, my voice moves through the distance of her dreams, calling: *Light, Light*.

I lift her and feed her and as we prepare to leave the house, I do something I never did for her brothers. With her fluffy tangle of toddler hair, her inherited shorts and t-shirt, she looks just like them, until I force her hair into tight, tidy ponytails. She squeals and complains and smacks my fingers away, and still, I am compelled to tug her into girlishness. In the mirror that holds both of us, my dark hair shadows her fair, and there, I observe her reflected scowl at her mother: a real little girl.

It doesn't take long to drive the children to our destination: a warehouse in an industrial estate. Even from the car park, I can hear the screams that rise from within. I slam the boot. I loathe this place. I force myself to come here and force myself to smile. The doors slide shut. Inside, the volume is close to unbearable. Everywhere, children are screaming, children are running and falling and weeping and laughing and screaming and screaming and screaming. The roof feels very far away, its metal joists punctuated with long silver tubes. Below, I stand bewildered in a mistranslated castle that merges a foam-brick turret with a plastic-ball moat and netted chambers stacked three storeys high. I can nearly read a spiral staircase into the configuration of one corkscrew slide – its exterior may be neon-yellow, but it is very dark inside. Through this nightmare vision, fleeting figures blur by, one girl's pink sweater morphing into another's green shirt: glimpsed, then gone. My sons are somewhere among this screeching flock, reckless in hellish merriment, laughing and slamming into other children, leaving them bloody-nosed and weeping, or limping and bleeding themselves.

I set myself at the edge of the dungeon where toddlers are sliding into a deep pit of plastic rainbow balls. A clutch of parents hovers there, each staring at their own child. My daughter bounces through, then wades back and flops onto my knee, rosy-cheeked and laughing. I want to remember this, so I tilt my phone and hold it at arm's length like an antique looking-glass. She smiles at my reflected smile, then darts away, leaving only a blur in the photo, and my face, fixed, peering after her. I press delete while she is scrambling back into the ball-pit, giggling, leaping, diving deep, then emerging with glee, having happened upon one large foam ball, a trespasser, squidgy and special among the identical others, and I smile at her delight, until I notice a younger boy wobbling beyond her. He is weeping, his hand opening and opening. My daughter's eyes follow my gaze and return, seeking guidance. Should she run, holding her precious discovery clutched to her breast? Or should she give it away for another's sake? I am torn between wanting to encourage her, and wanting to save her from becoming like me.

—

I think of all the ponytails that have lain in the post-box on Main Street. There may even be a new one there today, as ordinary as the post-box itself. In that dim metal chamber, carpeted and wallpapered with sacking, a slot of sun is interrupted only by the arrival of more mail. Tucked into one brown envelope, among all the other letters and parcels, is a ponytail. Rewind it.

See its envelope soar up through the slot and back into a girl's fist, to be pressed again to her chest. Now, she skips backwards down the street and into a salon again. Un-ding the bell. Reverse her into that room with all its tongs and aerosols, all its combs and blades. There, the envelope is un-licked and its address unwritten, letter by letter vanishing: L-E-Z-N-U-P-A-R. A pat is lifted twice from the child's head: 'girl. Good'. The grin slides off her mouth just as she slides back into the chair. In the mirror, her eyes bind to her mother's once more. The twin blades of the scissors are opening and opening, and she un-blinks, watching strands bind back to themselves, until her ponytail is long and unbroken again. Next, the straightener slides up and up, and her curl returns. Handful follows handful, the braids are re-braided. The silver cloak is un-flipped from her shoulders, the door is shut, and she is back on the street, long braids swaying at her waist.

What is it to consider oneself a donor – what does it cost us, and how do we gain from it? Having been puzzled by such muddy urges in myself, I often wonder at the ways in which the same impulses occur in others. My screen has led me to witness many similar moments: those who choose to suffer surgery in order to give a kidney to a stranger, for example, women injecting themselves in order to donate their eggs, or those who donate many hours of their lives to train guide-dogs. My own small efforts seem so prim by comparison, as I scroll and click their generosity in envy, wishing I could make myself as useful as others do.

On Rapunzel's Facebook page, girls grin from a triptych of photos that is almost always the same, though the faces and backgrounds change. In the first picture, every Emily, Alanna, Aoife, and Emma, every Ella and Lucy, is photographed grinning around the gaps in her teeth, with hair shining all the way to her waist. In the second image the hair is bound; the blade is visible. In the third, her hair is so short that she seems a different girl, holding her newly shorn pony-tail aloft like a record fish, her cheeks turned balloons of blush-pride. Her hair will be sent to a charity that creates bespoke wigs for those in need. In the pixels of all those child-eyes, I recognise a glint I know well, and wonder what they will give of themselves next.

The hair in the post-box is a beginning, and like any beginning, it holds promise beyond the visible. The DNA embedded in shorn hair is a variant called mtDNA, a mitochondrial substance inherited exclusively from the female parent. Although a mother passes this matter to all her children, only her daughters will pass it to the subsequent generation. This ordinary ponytail – drawn and drawn again through the straightener's hot blades – holds a direct female line.

—

While my thoughts have been tangling elsewhere, my child has made up her own mind. The weeping stranger weeps no more. He cuddles the ball to his belly and waddles away, dribble-grinning, while my daughter plops into the ball pit, despondent, her hands empty. I lift her and kiss her freckled cheek. 'Good girl,' I say. My mouth is salt; I hadn't noticed her tears.

Later, I lie next to her in the dark until she is asleep. The door falls closed behind me as I stand under the hall light, blinking at my reflection, my fingers tidying the black jumble of my hair. Apart. Two mirrors reflect us separately, now: a little dark in the light, and a little light in the dark.

9. blood in mud

M'fhada-chreach léan-ghoirt
ná rabhas-sa taobh leat

An ache, this salt-sorrow of mine,
that I was not by your side

—Eibhlín Dubh Ní Chonaill

THERE IS NOTHING IN LIFE that I want so badly as
to visit Eibhlín Dubh's marital home, Raleigh House.
This, I suspect, is the missing jigsaw piece that I need
to let go of her life and move on with my own. In the
absence of a name for the current residents, I address
a letter to the house itself. The house does not reply.

For weeks, every time my letterbox raps, I hop
up in hope, then slump in disappointment. I have
failed again. I resort to feeding my obsession through
my screen instead, squinting at satellite maps and
seeking out old images of the house's façade. I know
it's wrong to pry, but I can't help myself. Possession

works both ways; every time I google Eibhlín Dubh's home, something ugly in me whines: *Let me in.* I download black-and-white photos and zoom until I see it, still fixed to the wall – the eagle that followed Art home from Europe.

—

On 25 August 1768, Eibhlín's body howled open and her first son was born. He was given an inherited name, one shared by Art's brother and father – Conchubhar. The fact that his date of birth was etched on Art's gravestone allows me a rare accuracy that is absent from so much of my clumsy detective work. On finding such a clue, one is faced with the choice of what to do with it.

A revoltingly nosy woman might take it to the internet. In wondering whether Eibhlín Dubh was pregnant before her wedding, she might seek a website that calculates conception dates in reverse, engaging an algorithm of probability to discover the following:

> Most probable conception dates:
> 28 November – 2 December 1767
> Most probable dates of sexual intercourse
> that led to the pregnancy:
> 25 November – 2 December 1767

In pressing *Return*, such a woman might feel shame. She might ask herself (again) why she is clattering around in the intimate life of a stranger, without permission. Such doubts have been drawing question marks in the margins of my days for some time, though I try to ignore them. *What are you doing here?* those question marks seem to demand, and *Who will gain from this labour?* Not I, exhausted and googling conception calculators at 3:15 AM. Not Eibhlín Dubh, either, for I am beginning to suspect that none of this quest is truly to her benefit. In death, she would hardly worry over how her life is portrayed by academics. Through all my doubts, the nurse's voice continues its irritating loop: 'So what's all this for, then?'

—

Soon, another child was born to Eibhlín Dubh, a boy whose date of birth goes un-noted, sparing him the indignity of future busybodies and their internet calculators. Within three years of her marriage, Eibhlín's father had died. A year later, Art's father died too. During these years of griefs and joys, of births and deaths, Art came and went from his regiment in Europe. Eibhlín was often alone; Eibhlín was never alone.

By the spring of 1771, leaves were opening around Raleigh House again, and the air lilted with the giggle and screech of two little boys, the chatter of hens, and the warm whinny of horses. Eibhlín was pregnant with their third child when Art returned for the last time, dressed in his 'slender boots of foreign leather, / and the suit of fine couture / stitched and spun abroad for you'. She took pride in her lover's appearance, how even wealthy merchants' wives desired him. As their eyes followed Art, so too, I imagine, did their husbands'. Mary must have feared for her twin, for the reckless ways in which Art's swagger drew attention to all of them. She, too, must have observed the dark that was beginning to gather. Did she feel helplessness in the face of inevitability, as I do? In writing their lives from this distance, I am haunted both by the sense of looming catastrophe and by my own complicity, for in recounting this horror I must inflict it all over again. I wish I could stop the pain this telling will soon cast over Eibhlín Dubh, but I can't. The past never ends. Or, worse, the past tells us how it ends. Over, it says, over and over again.

—

This afternoon finds you in your car. You are by yourself. (This is a lie. You haven't been by yourself in some time.)

You are alone, though, and unspeakably tired. The plot you began has whittled ten pounds from your frame and carved dark hammocks under both of your eyes. You cannot continue like this, and yet, you can't sense an end to it either. Every radio tune seems to sing your strife, now, just as they did when your teenage heart first broke. You find yourself singing along to all the irksome lyrics you know by heart, in spite of yourself, '... and you give yourself away, and you give, and you give ...' and it's true, you have been giving yourself away, in donating your very thoughts and days to another. Your foot on the brake brings the car to a halt, askew in the margin. Your brow sinks to the wheel, and again, you weep. You idiot: there is no one to blame for this mess but yourself. You chose this path as blithely as a musician picks a sheet of music, giving herself to the precise choreography of movement and sound plotted by a stranger long before. Let it play you to its ending, foolish harpist. Prepare the strings.

—

An ill omen for one may be fortuitous for another. Among those who loathed Art was Abraham Morris, a formidable man who had once been high sheriff of Cork. His hatred was reciprocated.

On a warm Saturday in mid-July, the sound of hooves cantered through birdsong and honeysuckle-scented air. Art swung himself from his saddle in front of Hanover Hall, heels landing firmly on the drive. As he strolled up to the home of his enemy, his horse watched, her bridle speckled with spittle, her sides heaving. Art's fist thumped the heavy door. Both versions of what followed are recorded in writing, as each party subsequently published accounts in *The Cork Evening Post*. On 7 October, Morris's report stated:

> Whereas Arthur Leary of Raghleagh, a fellow of character most notoriously infamous, did, in the evening about 9 of the clock, on Saturday the 13th July last make an attempt on my life at my dwelling house in Hanover-Hall, and wounded one of my servants, and feloniously took from him a gun my property which he carried off for which crimes and several others the said Leary now stands indicted in the Crown Office of this court. Now, I do promise a reward of £20 to any person who will apprehend the said Leery and lodge him in the county gaol within twelve months of this date.

This notice effectively made of Art a wanted man, and put a price on his head. Within three days Morris's fellow magistrates in the Muskerry Constitutional Society convened a meeting and nodded their decision. Another notice was soon published, confirming Art's status as an outlaw in the eyes of the magistrates. A fortnight later, a reply from Art appeared in the same newspaper, noting that –

having occasion to apply to Mr Morris, as a magistrate relative to some law proceedings, he did for that purpose about 7 o'clock in the evening of July 13th last, repair to Hanover-Hall, the seat of Mr Morris, and there in a very modest and respectful manner communicate to him the purport of his complaint, and who without the least cause of provocation fell into a furious rage, and made use of very indecent, abusive, and ungentlemanlike language to the said Leary, who thereupon quitted his house and was returning home.

Before he got down the avenue he observed Mr Morris and John Mason his servant each armed with a gun, pursuing him down the avenue, and when Mr Morris advanced within twenty yards of the said Leary, he presented his gun at, and shot and wounded him in the hand, whereupon the said John Mason advanced close up to said Leary and presented his gun at him, which said Leary most providentially wrested from him before he had time to perpetuate that crime in the commission of which his master not intentionally failed and afterwards committed the same gun into the hands of one of his Majesty's Justices of the Peace, and soon after lodged an information against this Mr Morris for the violent assault and attack upon his life.

A reader might be forgiven a certain scepticism in both tellings of this event. Despite the price on his head, Art ran his mare in local races, where she won over the other horses, including one owned by Morris.

Enraged, his enemy demanded that Art acquiesce to the Penal Laws by selling her for the humiliating (and legal) sum of £5. Art, being Art, lashed Morris with his whip, daring him to a duel. Morris – being Morris – refused.

—

On 4 May Art was leaving Raleigh, when he –

> turned back swiftly
> and kissed your two babies.
> Heart of the palm, your kiss for me,
> and when you said, 'Rise, Eibhlín,
> settle your affairs neatly,
> be firm about it, move quickly.
> I must leave the home of our family,
> and I may never return to ye,'
> oh, I only chuckled in mockery,
> since you'd made such warnings so frequently.

Art left. He had decided that this would be the day to confront Morris once and for all. First, though, he would stop for a quick drink. Or several. As he drank, Art's plan was overheard. The eavesdropper drained his glass and rode ahead. Morris smiled at his informant. He had already made an outlaw of Art. Now he could act with impunity.

—

Hoof-song drummed Art merrily along his path, but on entering the village of Carriganima, he slowed. Something felt ... awry. His soldier's eye scanned the text of the village, translating any peril that might be lurking there. Yes. There were men crouching ahead. A trap. Art's heart quickened; mine does too. He turned away from the road and crept towards the stream instead, easing the bit across his mare's tongue, turning her head and hooves to skid those moss-slimed stones and up the bank, his ankles urging her onwards through the grasses. Only then did he pause to look back. Ha! He had done it! He had outwitted them, the bastards, he had side-stepped their trap. His horse tugged her head high as he laughed and yelled insults at Morris with glee.

Among those glaring back was a one-eyed soldier named Green. He held an old musket wedged between clavicle and jawbone. Within his weapon was a single ball of lead, stuffed firm by wadding and powder, pushed, primed and ready. Morris shouted one word. FIRE. Every soldier squeezed a trigger. Through the roar and the smoke, only one musket-ball reached Art, lodging with a shock in the warm meat of his body. Green's fingers quivered, releasing the clenched metal as others patted him rough congratulations.

Art's mare strained to lift him to safety, but blood was pouring from his wound, his fingers were opening, and Art was falling, falling, a fistful of her mane tearing away as he fell. That wet length of hair was all he held as he lay in the dirt, his gaze dashing wildly in its final flashes – *clouds, thick and close – blackthorn blossoms jigging in the breeze – a hoof – a pair of starlings hurrying elsewhere.* The mare looked down at her master, then back to the laughing soldiers, strolling ever closer. Do animals weigh self-preservation against selflessness? This mare chose her path quickly. Some urge turned her, tail high, wind-whipped, to canter away, her reins long and loose. She stumbled, then sprawled a long leap over the hedge, galloping, now, galloping and galloping.

With a final kick to Art's rib, Morris's men left. Their laughter left with them. The mare was hurrying away too, froth flying from her bit. She knew who was needed.

—

The horse who is galloping through our thoughts now is a female being, conceived, born, and reared in Europe.

Look: the stable is dawn-dark and straw-hush, and through this gloom, we watch her birth, swimming hoof-first from the warm ocean of her mother's body. Little footling, her hooflets are waves, dashing wildly against the earth, amazed. Her mother nudges her, nostrils quivering, until the foal opens her eyes and stands. The foal grows before our eyes. She thrives. In meadow sunshine, she need only nuzzle her mother's udder to release a rush of sweet milk. With her first gallop, she gives herself to the bliss of speed and the rush of the breeze. She is of solid stock, as bright and as quick as any of her foremothers. Through each generation of her family, a human voice has echoed the same words in a series of tongues: *Good girl. Good girl.*

Once weaned, she is schooled in servitude. Her life's purpose, she sees, will be to bear a human weight, and she learns it quick, the ways of stirrup and bit, of rein and whip. She is soon sold from her mother's presence; never again will she meet those dark eyes. Instead, she comes to know the crisp straw of cavalry stables, the swhisht and clang of swords, the tang of muskets, the smell of blood in mud, blue-bell shade under a beech tree, and autumn apples. This horse is glory and servant, she is speed and death sentence, and she performs each of her roles impeccably. Oblivion: eventually, she will draw death on her master. Then, in reciprocity, his death will lead to her own.

No matter how many times the *Caoineadh* galloped from mouth to mouth, no matter how many academic works respond to it, one detail is always missing. We never learn this horse's name. I cannot bring myself to invent one. Instead, I honour her among The Unnamed, a further absence among all the other female absences that are missing from this tale.

I want you to know that she was a female being.
I want you to know that she was a female, being.
I want you to know that she was.

—

The sole mercy I can send from my life to Eibhlín Dubh's lies in how I choose to unspool the following events. So for a moment, let me gift her some ordinary peace. I could draw her dozing, a cheek resting on her arm. I could draw her writing a letter, winding a clock, or scolding a small boy. Instead, I draw her with her favourite blue vase, poking rose stems among the freesias. I try to let this moment linger as long as I can, but all too soon, inevitability intrudes. Some leaf-flash draws her gaze to the window. Some stray hoof-syllable frets her brow. *Tick* goes her clock, *tick tick*, and in the yard, then, she sees – *reins* – *trailing*

– *wet* – *saddle* – *empty*. When she meets the horse's eye, she is quick to translate her gaze. What does she do, then? Does she seek help? Does she send a messenger to the Baldwins? Does she summon a servant to alert a magistrate? No. Eibhlín, our Eibhlín, does not pause to think. She leaps.

> Three leaps, I took – the first to the threshold,
> the second to the gate,
> the third to your mare.

Gripping the horse by fist and by knee, she gallops, she gallops, they both gallop for forty minutes or more, the exhausted mare heaving herself uphill over wet ground and down through crumpling pebbles and puddles. Eibhlín Dubh knows neither their destination nor what awaits her as the horse bounds through the river Sullane and the Foherish, as she trots the muddy paths between brambles and under branches, through pastures and streams and cow shit. Who watches them, as they go? The crows. The crows know. In such moments roadside furze always seems to blur, but Eibhlín holds tight, she grips the beast. On she goes, on and on and on – until she stops. Every time I read the following verse, my heart breaks again for her.

Fast, I clapped my hands,
and fast, fast, I galloped,
fast as ever I could have,
until I found you before me, murdered
by a hunched little furze
with no Pope, no bishop,
no clergy, no holy man
to read your death-psalms,
only a crumpled old hag
who'd draped you in her shawl-rag.
Love, your blood was spilling in cascades,
and I couldn't wipe it away, couldn't clean it
    up, no,
no, my palms turned cups and oh, I gulped.

Who is this crumpled bystander? To me, this elderly stranger sometimes feels like a manifestation of Eibhlín herself, returned in old age as a powerless witness who cannot change anything, who can only root herself there until her own young self hurries in, her body filled still with the stirrings of an infant who will never live. She watches her own young self falling, howling over Art's corpse until those vowels falter and begin to take form as words, words that somehow summon the voice of her mother, and her mother's mother, a whole chorus of female voices from her throat, all articulating the pain of this moment, all hand in hand in hand, all hovering in the rapture of those old words. Some alchemy turns this private moment public, turns a raw sound into articulation, into art. The horse hears that animal howl and understands, her forelock falling to her fetlock, her hoof scraping the ground.

The mysterious old woman is not only Eibhlín Dubh's older self, however. She is also you, and she is me. We are both bound in that peculiar figure too; we peer through her eyes, we are wrapped in her dark cloak. We bend together to spread it over Art's body. We give of ourselves to shelter him. We stand with her to grieve him. This stranger holds all of us. I will not allow Eibhlín Dubh to suffer this alone, nor will you. Let us step in and stand with her. We cannot permit reason to intrude upon this moment. Do not deny us this.

—

The first night of aftermath is darker than dark. Art's horse is absent. Hours before, she was tugged away by a stranger, and though she whinnied her European curses, no one noticed the dwindling pendulum of her hooves.

The door of the mill is ajar, with candle-light flickering from the gap. Two men have hauled the strongest door in the village off its hinges, shouldered it here and set it over a pair of barrels, then lifted Art's body and laid him on it – a generous gesture. Eibhlín sits on a rickety stool, her body rocking. Her husband's left hand is clutched in her fingers, while his right hand lies open over an empty keyhole. She knows that she cannot expect her mother's firm embrace, and yet with each creak of the door, she can't help but glance up.

Art's jaw has fallen open, but his eyes are closed. Rain sneaks through the roof to drip a metronome in the corner. It grows colder. By the wall, a cluster of mill-women stand, dark-shawled and serious. Eibhlín resents them for not weeping with her: 'and to multiply my thousand cataclysms, / not one of them will summon a tear for him'. The rain falls. The rain falls faster. Listen: the drips tick-tick-tick over the whispers of strangers, the intermittent sniffling, the muffled condolences, and then, towards the door, one by one the sorrow-nodders go, to huddle outside with raised brows and rumours tilting ear to mouth, ear to mouth. Beyond, the river hums its old song.

Eibhlín's right hand twitches to her full-moon belly, but her left hand remains with his, for as long as she holds her grip, her warmth will keep the cold from his limb. Now, her spine straightens. Now, she will begin. Now, those words again, those begun on the hill, when her chin was still wet-red from him, when only an animal and a stranger stood with her. Now her mouth opens, and the cold mill with its audience of farmers, gossipers, mill-women, and strangers grows silent, but for her voice.

—

But for her voice, I would be spending Sunday afternoon at home with my family, playing hide and seek, watching an old film, or carving roast chicken. Instead, I've left my daughter to sleep in her father's arms again, snug and warm with a belly full of milk. I slow near a bric-a-brac shop, parking by a selection of items propped on the roadside: a fireside chair, a child's bike, and several old gates. Here I am, I think, as my door slams a clutch of starlings over the rooftops of Carriganima – I may be an inept detective, but I am a devoted servant.

I have exhausted myself lately, absenting myself from my own days to seek the days of another, and I have begun to feel troubled by my behaviour, questioning whether my attempts are really any more useful than the abrupt lines of biography that first provoked me. How dare I pry on the private moments of a life, stitching frills where the pattern calls for no such thing? My daydreams have choreographed rainfall on this village, sliding it into the mill in which Eibhlín Dubh keened, despite holding no evidence of the actual weather that evening. If my desire to make her feel true makes of her a marionette then that makes me ... what? I roam the street in search of some remnant of the flour mill, sneaking down driveways and behind sheds, with raindrops dampening my face. I walk the length of the village again, trying and trying to find some remnant of that structure. Again, I fail. I fail her, I fail you, and I fail myself.

Shivering and glum, I turn to the only open door I can find. Beyond the roadside bric-a-brac a sign reads THE OLD CURIOSITY SHOP. Inside, the room is filled with crooked limbs of old furniture, football memoirs, gas lamps, mirrors, and sewing machines. The drizzle deepens to rain, knocking on the roof with a desire I recognise: *let me in, let me in.* A man pops his head around the corner, waves, then disappears again. My palm lingers on the cracked glass of a tall clock, the tiny jagged splinterings of its chest, its empty keyhole, its door ajar. I reach in to set its pendulum swinging, then notice a chipped side-plate beyond it, full-moon pale with a village inked in vivid blues, where a tiny couple wanders by a stream. Lost. A plump vase nearby glows blue as the autumn tides at Derrynane. Both the vase and the plate cost me a total of three coins: I smile as I leave.

Outside, the rain has lifted and the stream sings icy welcomes to my toes as they slip over the stones. This water must have driven the mill-wheel once, its liquid lunge sending the same circle around and around. *Listen*, the stream says. *ListenListenListenListen*. I do – or at least, I try to.

—

At Derrynane, should a girl grow lost or fearful, she might find her bearings by turning her head to the compass pin of the tide's thrum, or by calling out to her twin for help. We do not know whether Mary held her sister's hand in the mill. It seems unlikely, given that an entire verse of the *Caoineadh* curses her husband, 'that shit-talking clown, / that bockety wimp, all mean frowns'. What could he have done to provoke such intense loathing? Mrs O'Connell writes approvingly, 'Mr. Baldwin had the mare given up, which in the then state of the laws was the wisest thing he could have done for the widow and children.' Wise, perhaps. Cruel, too. At some point in the early hours of her raw-throated grief, Eibhlín raised her face, red-eyed and exhausted, to be told that Art's beloved mare had been given to the man who had ordered his murder.

—

Each autumn, when leaves begin to dream of gold, the night-tide at Derrynane shimmers neon blue. It swells with phytoplankton, each wave bustling tiny phosphorescent particles until specklets glimmer bright and brighter, then slowly grow dull again. For a human eye to perceive such bioluminescence, the night must be deeply dark.

After Art's burial, Eibhlín lies in the dark of a bedchamber far inland, singing her sons to sleep. Soon she is the only one awake; only then does salt spill over her cheeks. What will happen next, Eibhlín does not know – but we do. Death beckons to death. Overhead, the shadows of dark birds loom.

—

At home, I am struggling to compose myself in the darkness that spills from Eibhlín Dubh's life. I try to distract myself in my routine of sweeping, wiping, dusting, and scrubbing. I cling to all my little rituals. I hoard crusts.

Every day, I fall to my elbows and beckon more crusts from under tables and high chairs, crawling through banana goo, yoghurt, and crushed grapes.

That I move through my days with grimy knees is worth it to retrieve these crescents of bread, still spit-wet, moulded by gum and by fist, because it is these crusts that allow me the strangest and most precious moment of the day, when I will hear my name fly from a crow's mouth.

I spill a box of jigsaw pieces in front of the children, then turn my back on their diligent fingers to walk into the garden. Cool and plush, the carpet of this green room. A sentry's neck tilts immediately towards the pad-pad of my bare feet, her squint-eye translating my tangle of unbrushed hair into the name they have given me. She opens her beak to roar that split-syllable across the valley, and I watch them all lift from parlours of twig, surging towards me by screech and by wing, yelling dark greetings.

When the government announces a nationwide snowstorm alert, TV bulletins display empty bakery shelves; now everyone hoards bread as I do. At breakfast, I can't bring myself to chew my toast. My stomach squawks when I sip black coffee instead, feeling each hot mouthful grow wings inside me, lush and dark.

Even the smallest hungers can feed others. Viewed from above, our snowy garden must appear white as a page, and there I stand, a female silhouette, my middle hunger-snipped, as overhead, a hundred wings scissor a gale.

10. two roads,
each blurred

Buail-se an bóthar caol úd soir
mar a maolóidh romhat na toir,
mar a gcaolóidh romhat an sruth,

Hit that narrow road east
where each tree will kneel for you,
[and] each stream will narrow for you,

—Eibhlín Dubh Ní Chonaill

I. PASSENGER AS DRIVER

In the night-city, it's easy to blot out the dark. Here, the haloes of street lamps are set so close to one another that their amber glow falls unbroken through our car, a steady light that spills over the steering wheel and over my love's hand, tinting the wedding ring he had engraved with my name.

I like to sit aside when he drives – I like to watch his hand, the hand around which he will soon twist my ponytail as he tugs my head back to kiss me. I like to watch his face too, the smile that grows there when he feels my eyes on him, knowing that soon we will reach the rooms in which our children sleep, and the walls against which he will push me until I moan into his palm. The night that I first pressed my lips to his, we were both nineteen, and although a year had passed since I'd been yanked back from the river-railings, my hair was still damp. With him, at last, I began to laugh. He entered my life with neither fanfare nor glamour. There was no elopement. He simply fell into step by my side, with his easy smile, his old t-shirts, his worn jeans, and his steady footfall. Now we are driving the same road we walked hand-in-hand as teenagers, faster still.

Approaching the suburbs, the lights grow more broadly spaced. I watch pools of darkness move over his face; how quickly they seep and dissipate. We hurry together through those small darks, a little late for the babysitter, and a little hungry for each other. The car is still lit intermittently from beyond, but the darker pools grow longer, now. I don't notice which light is the last.

Our headlights are useless at the T-junction, their twin yellows staring ahead, illuminating only a knot of brambles. Instinct or habit tugs our heads to the left, to the right, and to the left again in vigilance, although we can't see anything through the solid dark that shoves itself against the glass. In the absence of any approaching lights, he drives on. I tremble when the dull roar of the engine shudders us onwards into the unseeable. I'm not sure I can wait until we get home for his fingers, and maybe, I think, maybe I could ask him to find some quiet gateway, some secret spot where we could – just for a minute – but now we are rounding a bend, and now he is slamming the brakes, and now our car is screeching to a neck-aching halt.

We both hold our hands high, flimsy shields against that sudden light. Neither of us speaks, though both of us see the man standing next to a taxi, his face empty, while another car's hazard lights blare crimson to dark and dark to crimson. Beyond the man I see another man, or maybe two, each with phones to their ears, and below them, now, I notice something else. Someone. A silhouette, splayed flat across the white line. A silhouette in miniskirt and stilettoes. A silhouette that is writhing. A woman.

This blind slope, where the road twists so steeply at both neck and ankle, is the most treacherous place I could imagine for a young woman to lie alone in the dark. 'No,' says my husband. 'NO. Do not,' but *tick* goes my seatbelt and *tick-tick* goes the door handle. 'No,' he says again, 'people are already helping,' but my body is rising now, leaping from the car, and perhaps a better wife would obey, allowing others to resolve this unknown crisis, perhaps a better person would let herself be driven away, but I can no longer hear his voice, because I am running through the darkness, now, running and kneeling and touching this stranger's shoulder, asking her name.

I see no blood, no broken bone, but she is howling and rocking, rocking, rocking side to side. Tyres screech another vehicle to a skewed halt behind ours, and when I glance back, I think I see my husband's shadow flinch in his seat. The taxi driver approaches, lifting his arms in a loud shrug, palms up to absolve himself, talking fast, 'I didn't touch her, I swear, when I picked her up she was fighting with her fella, she clattered him square in the face, and then he kicked her, right in the' – his finger towards his crotch – 'and she just jumped in then, bawling, you know, and when I slowed down to ask if she was alright, she threw herself out the door, and I can't leave her there, can I, but I can't drag her into the car either if she won't go, and' – his phone rings and he turns to answer, still grumbling over his shoulder as he goes – 'she's going to kill us all with this carry on, the selfish b— Hello? Yeah, listen, I'll be with you as soon as—'

The woman utters no discernible words, but there is a low howl held between her chattering teeth. I am gripped by the mother-urge to hold, to comfort, to shield, but most of all by the urge to recite the magic words that always press reset, that always conjure calm from panic. I lift her face in my hands, find her eyes with mine, and say, 'Everything will be OK.' I ease her sad body up and steer her along, my palm very gentle at her elbow. As we walk together through the dark, my ears and eyes are on high vigilance, terrified as I am that a car might round the bend too fast to stop. I know I can't fix her but I do what I can, I settle her safely into the car, I stroke her hair until her sobs ease. I ask if she needs the hospital and she shakes her head. I ask if she wants to go home, if she feels safe in the cab, and she nods, so I click her seatbelt, slam the door, and never see her again.

When I return to our car my fingers are shaking too much to fumble my own seatbelt into its latch, so my husband shoves it in with an exasperated sigh. He is angry. 'That girl was so drunk she won't even remember you tomorrow. You could have killed us,' he says, 'and for what?' I want to ask why he didn't help too, but before he has even turned the key, a van veers past, making of our car a flimsy echo of its speed. I see it clearly, then: in abandoning him here, on this blind bend, to run into the dark – fearless, or foolhardy, or both – my actions had put both of us at risk. To him, I was merely interrupting a situation that was already under control: there were others there who would surely have resolved the whole mess. I had seen something very different in those male shadows as they fell over a woman sprawled on the ground. Turning the key, his lips are tight white.

The rarity of his anger makes it startling. I apologise and we drive on in silence. I wonder why these urges are embedded in me: the quick apology, yes, but also the desire that might surge up at any moment, faster than synaptic flash, sending me sprinting into the dark, too quick to be thwarted by shouts of reason. In attempting to do the right thing for one, I endanger another; in my efforts to help a stranger, I jeopardise both my husband and my children. I hadn't even paused to consider them. Even now, as our car gathers speed, I am buzzing with the sparkle of achievement, the delight of donating my small assistance to another, the thrill of giving a kindness and expecting nothing in return. I don't, however, feel that I can take any credit for my actions – it felt almost as though I was being driven into the dark by some force too powerful to resist. How mysterious, our instincts, those sudden engines that roar up to steer us towards new ends.

All the way home, I puzzle over his question, 'and for what?' I am still thinking about it as we brush our teeth, as he wraps his arms around me and kisses my neck, then falls asleep. In the dark, I realise that there is only one way I could cast this incident as transactional, but it's far too esoteric to reveal to him, and besides, I can't bring myself to wake him. Let me tell you, instead. Perhaps it was the familiarity of giving myself away that first made me leap from the car, but in the moment that I bent towards that road, it was dark – dark as a river – dark enough to set some old sensation stirring in me. In helping that stranger up, maybe I was a shadow twin of the stranger who once heaved my own weeping, drunken self back from the railings of another river in another night. In rocking her, maybe I was rocking my own old aching self. Maybe there was some equivalence embedded in that moment, some weird reciprocity. In whispering to a stranger that everything would be OK, maybe I was casting a spell over all of us in our sorrow and pain, over her pain, and his pain, and mine, and maybe it was true, maybe it really would be OK, this time. Maybe it already was.

II. DRIVER AS PASSENGER

Much later, another Friday night finds me alone and moving fast, deep under a river. Down here, all is bright, even when the world above is dark. I imagine what stirs unseen beyond the tunnel: the layers of squelching murk and all the fast gallons of liquid, swerving its cargo of trout and pike, so many eyes, so many hearts hurried through the hurrying river, while moonlight dances briefly on its surface. Underneath, I am blazing through a tunnel of dazzling fluorescence, my radio so loud that the bass throbs behind my breastbone. Once the tunnel begins to slope west, my foot meets the pedal again, rushing me into the night.

I've been invited home to give a reading from my poems, so I am following this road back to the small, wet fields where countless incarnations of my family have found themselves waking up, morning after morning, day after day, century after century. Magnet-fast, I flash past signs that all repeat each other – [SLOW] [SLOW] [SLOW] – past dark windows, past the glimpsed hill-silhouette of two horses who doze in tree-shadow. This is the way home. My momentum is very recent; the fastest my grandmother's mother could have moved was gallop speed. Through miles and miles of night countryside, my four wheels spin blank as clock-faces, and above, a thin metal vessel is filled with heat and music and one warm body with one small heart pulsing and one mouth filled with song: me.

Swift, the twist from ordinary to catastrophe. In eerie slow motion I grasp that the lights approaching me are not the innocuous beams from the opposite side of the motorway. No, these headlights are moving towards me. Wrong, I think, the wrong way. Time slows to a sharp clarity as the oncoming headlights swivel crimson, then white again. The car smashes against the central verge, spinning now, spinning wildly in chaotic circles across both lanes, allowing me to glimpse something else in motion behind it – another vehicle, also spinning – and I am minor and inconsequential, moving unstoppably towards two vehicles, both whirling like parallel entities in deep space, each spinning its own arc, while I careen towards them, gripping my wheel and gritting my teeth. The radio must be still playing, but I hear nothing. I hear nothing at all.

My body, sensing shock, switches itself to some long-buried incantation, whispering *Oh God Oh God Oh God Oh God*, my breath short, rasping. I am a splinter, a flimsy distillation of all the humans who collided in the haphazard pattern that eventually yielded me, a woman who birthed four children, who squandered her days in housework and daydream, a woman who lived for thirty-six years before steering herself into a grisly death on the motorway. My mind flashes to my children, tucked snug and dreaming, while downstairs my husband is sipping a beer and watching sports on TV, oblivious. My heart hurts.

Oh God. Oh God. My mouth is still moving when my car reaches the collision.

The first car is spinning faster now, as I skid an arc through the deep mud beyond the hard shoulder. My wheels spin and slip. I wince, feeling debris rolling and banging violently under the car, so many smashed fragments of plastic and metal and glass, all airborne, soaring under me on their path to embedding themselves in the margin. My car slips sideways as they pass below, the steering wheel tugging itself away from me fast as a slapped cheek. As my hands wrestle it back under control, my mind flies away, imagining whether a stranger will someday bend to that dirt, lift a splinter, and wonder at the moment that tore it from its whole. Still, I grip the wheel, still *Oh God, Oh God*, veering sharply into the periphery, still, the two cars are spinning, nudging each other, now, and if there are human shadows in those vehicles, I do not see them. I feel as though I am alone in this dark, my feet dancing on the pedals, swerving around a pair of revolving, empty cars.

Then, shockingly, I pass it. I have passed it, I think, I am past, I am on the other side, and somehow, somehow, I am alive. My hands are shaking uncontrollably, and I find that I am weeping, though I don't know when the tears began. The gasping continues, the incantation of *Oh God Oh God Oh God*. I force my mouth to stop. I inhale, indicate, cut the engine, and try to call emergency services. My hands are shaking so much that it takes three efforts before it rings.

An exceptionally calm woman notes my details, asks me to 'Please say that again.' My eyes dart as I speak, straining to the side and behind and ahead again, but it is so dark outside that I can't see a thing; my rear-view mirror feels both very empty and very full. When I ask her what I should do, I am giving myself away once more; I am putting my decision in her hands. When I ask her what I should do, I am weighing another sprint in the dark against the easy glide to another's direction. When I ask her what I should do, she knows the answer and delivers it with a firmness that is unequivocal. She forbids me from running back to the other cars. Instead, she orders me to drive on, 'Yes, now, immediately,' for fear of causing a further collision. She weighs my potential helpfulness against the danger I could present to others and tells me that I must leave.

I do as I'm told. *Good girl.* My knees are shaking, and the steering wheel keeps spilling through my slick palms. Perhaps it was never as clear as I imagined; perhaps we are each capable of choosing a different direction, depending on the road on which we find ourselves. Perhaps the kaleidoscopic versions of ourselves that inhabit our days and nights are capable, in fact, of anything. On this particular night, a calm voice tells me what to do and this time, I do not defy it. This time I see the sense in the command and I comply. I thank the voice on the phone. I say goodbye.

All my mirrors are bursting black. The consequences of denying my urges are excruciating. My desire to help doesn't disappear as I accelerate – it badgers me, blaring relentlessly in the dark through which I drive. Have I left someone howling behind me? Tomorrow, I will spend hours searching local news bulletins for any listing of a serious collision and find nothing, but I don't know that yet. Now, I make myself do as I'm told. On this road, I drive away.

11. blot. blot.

Thugas léim go tairsigh

Three leaps, I took – the first to the threshold

—Eibhlín Dubh Ní Chonaill

A FLEETING DISTRACTION from anguish may be found in devising a revenge. Or two.

At Raleigh House, Eibhlín Dubh was grieving. She was also plotting.

—

Quietly, fingers unbolt a stable door.
Quietly, so quietly, hooves are muffled by burlap sacks.
Quietly, the twine is tied, the rope tugged.

—

When Eibhlín Dubh welcomes the mare home, it is by gentling her brow to that of the beast: two faces, each held in the warmth of female breath.

Others, however, begin to worry. What punishment might Morris inflict upon discovering this theft? The sole defence anyone could suggest in these circumstances is concealment; such a problem must be hidden.

The shot sends a ricochet of sound galloping the courtyard walls. Again, the mare's legs shiver like a foal's, a slow crumpling that makes waves of her hooves once more, dashing against the earth. Again, the warm, wet spread of blood in mud. She grows still. Her body may now be buried anywhere, but her face cannot – with its unique markings, it could still identify her as Art's. So, the necessary separation, the blade, the back-and-forthing. The hearthstone is heaved aside like a door. By shovel blades, men dig the room in which her face must remain. Skull under stone: when Eibhlín sits by the fire, she is never alone.

—

Within weeks of the shooting, a coroner's inquest is convened. In opposition to previous assertions by the magistracy that the murder of this 'outlaw' was legitimate, the inquest asserts 'a verdict that Abraham

Morris and the party of soldiers were guilty of the wilful and wanton Murder of Arthur O Laoire'. All the soldiers involved – including Green, whose musket shot killed Art – are transported to what was then termed the 'East India Colonies'. Morris remains in Ireland, although he soon leaves the grandeur of Hanover Hall and secures temporary rooms in a city lodging house instead.

In a verse of the *Caoineadh* sometimes attributed to Art's father (who had, it seems, predeceased Art by several years), Eibhlín rails against the perpetrator of all her woes.

> Morris, you runt; on you, I wish anguish! –
> May bad blood spurt from your heart and
>   your liver!
> Your eyes grow glaucoma!
> Your knee-bones both shatter!
> You who slaughtered my bull-calf,
> and not a man in all of Ireland
> who'd dare shoot you back.

Perhaps revenge might be considered the opposite of altruism. Whereas the latter leaves a human interaction lopsided, vengeance demands a strict balancing of the equation. An eye for an eye. A tooth for a tooth.

—

The second retaliation occurred on 7 July, when Art's teenage brother Cornelius cantered the muddy roads and cobblestones that led to the sewer-stench of the city. He knew that Morris had rented rooms at Boyce's lodging house, so he chose a spot near Hammond Lane and leant discreetly against a wall. Time has rendered the shape of his weapon opaque – magistrates later stated that it may have been a musket under his coat, or perhaps a blunderbuss. As he watched the comings and goings from the lodging house, his finger traced cold metal. Daylight faded. By eleven, the summer night had lured a light to some windows and a drowsy darkness to others. Beyond those drapes, sleep was beginning to weave the strange fabric of human dream, while out on the street, Cornelius was yawning.

Inside, Morris was growing weary too. He climbed the stairs to his bedchamber, latched the door, and began to ready himself for sleep, as sounds of tipsy merriment rose from beyond the window. The moment that Cornelius glimpsed Morris's silhouette at the window, his heart broke into a gallop and his cheeks blazed. He took aim. Glass splashed its cold splinters into the bedroom, and Morris startled, staggering back. Several shots flew awry, embedding themselves just below his window, but one found its way into his body, piercing the warmth between ribcage and hip. Before Moriss's knees had even met the ground, before his first gasp for help, Cornelius was already sprinting away. His heart roared as he shoved through the muddy streets and dark laneways of the city, chest heaving, until he heard the low shush of river-waves on the docks. Soon, he was standing on the deck of a ship, turning his face towards the horizon. Perhaps salt-spray lashed his cheeks. Perhaps his cheeks were dry.

The magistrates were quick to issue a proclamation for Cornelius's capture. Among contemporaneous notices against those suspected of 'forcibly carrying away Arabella Allen, of CORK, spinster, with intent to marry her', and those 'who houghed the cattle of Thomas BUTLER, of Woodvill' is a proclamation 'against the persons who fired into the bed-chamber of Abraham MORRIS, of Hanover Hall, Co. Cork, Esq., at his lodgings in the City of Cork'. A substantial sum had been gathered from Morris's allies, including a sum of more than £45 from William Tonson, a sitting MP, and 100 guineas from Morris himself. Over subsequent months, the reward grew. Cornelius, however, had reached America, and would never return. Both brothers' voices were lost to the rooms of Raleigh forever.

Despite his wounds, Morris did not die. He lived to limp in to Art's murder trial and to limp away from his acquittal. On 6 September 1773, the *Cork Evening Post* declared, 'Last Saturday September 4th at Cork Abraham Morris was tried for the killing of Arthur O'Leary where he was honourably acquitted.' Morris may not have suffered official punishment for Art's murder, but he did suffer greatly with his wound; it never healed. For years, he must have wept through fever dreams and repeated infections and agonies, until he devised a plan to fund his recovery. His belongings would all be translated into cash. On 1 July 1775, an advertisement appeared in the *Cork Evening Post*:

> To be sold by auction at Hanover Hall the seat of Abraham Morris who is going away for the benefit of his health, all his household furniture, bullocks, cows, sheep, farming and other utensils.

What would he do with the money? Where would he go? Months later, a second notice was published:

> Cork: 25 September 1775: The creditors of Abraham Morris Esq. are requested to send in their demands to James Boyce of Hammond's Marsh where the speediest methods will be found to discharge same.

Any scholarship I find deduces that Morris died of complications from his wound two years after it was inflicted – an extravagantly slow and painful death. I can understand the basis of this deduction: why else would the landlord of Morris's lodging house be settling debts on his behalf? Nevertheless, I can't resist searching burial records for his name. I fail. I have yet to find evidence of Abraham Morris's death.

—

Three times, I have written begging letters to Raleigh House, but the house is quiet, the house won't reply. Finally, I confide in a kind librarian who takes pity on me, sending a friend he shares with the current occupant to plead on my behalf. The answer, when it comes, is indisputable: this woman wants to keep her private rooms private. Her door will never yield to my shoulder-bone. When I weep, I weep for me, I weep for you, and I weep for Eibhlín.

After the tears, however, I can't sleep for acid-guilt. I lie in the privacy of my bed and imagine how vexing it would be to have a stranger presume a right to intrude in one's home. I come to hate myself for the selfish arrogance of my repeated requests. Again, the illusion of control: I may not be able to rewind my clumsy intrusions into this woman's life, but I can control the ritual of gesture. In the dark, my screen is a candle.

Soon, the streets of Macroom will wake to bird-song. There will be footsteps, then a key in a keyhole. A hand will gather the objects I have chosen: white roses, freesias, lilac lisianthus and trachelium, carnations and chrysanthemums. Those stems will be bound in twine and cloaked in cellophane, then ribboned and stickered and driven to Eibhlín Dubh's door.

A knucklebone will rap.

Beyond, the sound of footsteps. The click of a key.

That door will open, if not to me, then to my gift: a bouquet and a note to say *Sorry*. This choreography purchases not only an apology, however. It also secures oblique entry. At Raleigh, my pale rosebuds will wink open in the dark. In an older darkness, the night air grows scented, too, where Eibhlín is sitting alone. Under her bare feet lies a hearthstone, and under that stone lies a skull, tender as a fallen rose petal.

At dawn, wet footprints follow me through our dew-drenched garden, where a crow watches me scissor a single stem. Snip. By sitting that flower in the vase that found me in Carriganima, my sly orchestration raises rose-scent simultaneously across time and place, both in my rooms and in Eibhlín's. This vase, so blue, matches the iridescent tide at Derrynane, which is in motion now, too.

Who is haunting who?

—

Eibhlín's brother Maurice – now master of Derrynane – remained unwilling to extend his forgiveness. As he saw it, Art's death had drawn ignominy on Eibhlín, and by association, on Derrynane. In June 1773, their brother Daniel wrote from France:

> *I learned the unhappy fate of poor Arthur O'Leary. I can't express how much I've been shocked by it. The short acquaintance I had with him gave me a more favourable opinion than I had at first conceived of him. I still foresaw that his violence and ungovernable temper would infallibly lead him into misfortune ... It's, however, no small comfort to be assured there remains some livelihood for his orphans and widow ... You are too generous to add to her misfortunes. I am sure you've ere now forgot that she ever offended you, and let you exert your friendship for her and children.*

I find no record of Maurice's reply to this letter. The purse of Derrynane supported many, but it would not be opened for this sister.

In August, just a month after Morris was shot, festivities were planned at Derrynane. Nancy, the twins' youngest sister, was to marry. There was no chance that Eibhlín Dubh could attend the celebrations, but Mary did, with her husband and her beautiful children and her travelling chests full of finery.

The decade since she had left Derrynane had seen her transformation into a glamorous lady of society. Mary was now known as the beautiful Mrs Baldwin of Clohina, noted for her refinement, for her grace, and for the elegance of her fashions. In the summer of 1773, she was thirty years old, mother to six, sparkling in company, and deeply sophisticated. The gown she chose for this occasion was so fine that she became the talk of the celebration. A century later, people still spoke of it, as Mrs O'Connell discovered –

> Old Miss Julianna O'Connell remembers old people telling her, when she was young, what a pretty creature Mrs. Baldwin was, and how beautifully dressed she used to be, particularly on some special occasion. She rather thought it was to Nancy's wedding that she came with her pretty daughter. Mother and child were both dressed in open, long-waisted silk gowns over blue satin quilted petticoats, and the loveliest lace cap was partly covering the golden hair she wisely did not powder. When her brother Dan saw the six children, he immediately claimed this little damsel and three of the prettiest as real O'Connells, whereas poor brother Baldwin laughingly observed he was only giving him the plain ones for Baldwins.

While her family laughed and danced at Nancy's wedding, Eibhlín Dubh was not in the room; she had left.

Through the following months, the letters make no further mention – none at all – of her or of her children. Such is the correspondence between brothers. We may perhaps infer, as Mrs O'Connell does, that Maurice was not swayed by Daniel's previous appeal for compassion, because three summers later, Daniel repeats his request. On 6 July 1776, he writes:

> *Were it possible you'd bring your heart to forget the faults of the unfortunate Widow Leary, charity and her misery and misfortunes call upon you for mercy. I wish it may be, cu'd be, but dare not urge it from a sense of her offences. However, from my dear Maurice's good heart anything may be expected. Follow but its dictates and I'll venture to affirm you'll forgive.*

A delicate balance, this, the tightrope between respecting a patriarch's righteous anger and encouraging the sheltering of a widow. Every time I read this letter, I worry over her brother's phrasing of 'her misery and misfortunes' and 'her offences'. Might we assume that he is referring to Art's death, and the loss of her pregnancy? Or had some new catastrophe befallen her in the intervening years? I cannot bring myself to inflict further suffering on Eibhlín. When I attempt to imagine these years of hers, I see only the blizzard of TV static. Mrs O'Connell is more hopeful, however. She suggests that an eventual reconciliation occurred between Eibhlín and her mother, that Máire 'forgave her ... on the plea that no woman could have been expected to resist the pleadings of so handsome and attractive a suitor'. Máire Ní Dhuibh understood the force of female desire.

———

By 1791, eighteen years after Art's death, Eibhlín appears for the last time in the family letters. No longer 'the unfortunate Widow O'Leary', she becomes 'our sister Nellie' again. At forty-eight years old, she is reduced to a pet-name, a quick scratch of a quill within a male text. I have never been able to find a date of death or gravestone for my beloved ghost, but each time I re-read her brothers' letters, I grieve the point at which her name disappears.

I try to imagine the small treasures of her days, all she saw and took joy in: watching her sons begin to run, to ride, to read, their faces lit with Art's old smile. The flight of bats and swallows. The branches reaching higher each year, their leaves turning gold, falling, and then budding green again. All the remembered fragments of her dreams, all her frustrations, her money worries, her lists, her days of egg-pains and brass-polishing, her days of stretching dinners to feed many mouths, her days of brave faces and darning, her days of no letters, of no word from sister or brother, her days of loneliness, her days of laundry. Her children, waving back at her from the garden, from their saddles, from carriages, always waving as they leave. They wave, her boys. They wave and wave.

12. omen – of planes and starlings

I. AFTERBIRTH/AFTERMATH

Through November dusk, I am pushing my sleeping daughter over the same city path Cornelius once ran, when I hear starlings. I see them, then – twenty, or more – claws clinging to a graffiti-scrawled hoarding ahead. Like a row of nightclub DJs, they tilt their necks and nod to the beat, then beak by beak, they set to remixing the soundscape. First, a remembered fire alarm, then a snatch of human speech, next a car's ignition mixed with the spinning vinyl of a falling bin lid, a lighter's snick-snick, fire alarm again, fire alarm, fire alarm, higher and higher, until their melody lifts pitch into a scream. Repeat. Repeat. They are raucous, these birds, and yet my daughter doesn't stir. I wonder whether she is weaving their song into her dream.

As I come closer they startle skyward: a murmuration in miniature, ink blots swirling on a deep page. Untranslatable: is this an ominous display, a warning to predators, or a joyous farewell to the day? What, exactly, are they trying to say? I pause, my neck growing stiff and strange. The sense of observing something so eerie rise over the city reminds me of something else. Something I haven't told you yet. Weeks before the doctor's wand slowed over my belly, an airplane shadowed this city, a vessel that didn't fly through the sky. It flew behind my eyes. I was the blue through which it lifted its human cargo, and although I didn't know it yet, that plane, as it moved through me, was an omen.

The dream always unspooled the same way. I found myself idly observing an airplane as it climbed over the city, rising at an angle that appeared ordinary but swiftly became wrong, an ascent that grew steep and steep and steeper still, until – horror – it flipped back on itself, and started to fall, upturned and flat, plunging fast, until it crashed, making of the street a puddle of flame. Every time it exploded, I jolted awake. Only now do I see how my body was trying desperately to wake me, by translating a deteriorating placenta into a visual language that might startle me into action. It didn't succeed; baffled though I was by this recurring dream-vision, I never asked myself whether there might be something to it. Every morning when I waddled, bleary-eyed, into the kitchen, my husband would kiss me and smile, 'Don't tell me – another plane?' Then off I'd go, tilting merrily into my list for the day, deleting word after word and task after task, each deletion an attempt to blot out the creeping sense of dread this dream left in its aftermath.

I never questioned the dream until I found myself lying by a hospital window, my cheek pressed to a damp pillow. I was alone. The blue I watched was punctuated only by an occasional bird and the roar and rush of airplanes, swooping towards the airport on the horizon. I watched those vessels land, one by one by one, delivering tourists safely to the same city I had dreamt, and then, I understood.

I remembered the doctors' eyes over their surgical masks the day before. They must have examined my failed placenta as a scholar might peer at a manuscript full of lacunae, seeking clues. Afterbirth: this red room, in its inaudible, inexplicable failure, had been the source both of my daughter's nourishment and of her peril. Only through our doctor's vigilance had this vessel succeeded in carrying its cargo into our world. What does an omen become if we thwart its forecasted doom? If harp strings split but no one perishes, who will tell of it?

When I think of the signs we are taught to fear – the single magpie, the broken mirror – I wonder at the scaffold that has fallen from each, the absent repercussion that first followed it. All our omens hold the mystery of some grave human consequence, now forgotten, leaving only the gleaming symbol in its aftermath. In attempting to comprehend a turn of ill-fortune, we may search for an omen as prelude, for to find such a sign imposes meaning on the chaotic. In seeking an omen, we frequently seek a bird.

In May 1622, a century and a half before Art's death, the city I dreamt was ablaze. Flames ripped through all its paths and rooms, demolishing nearly every structure it met, whether composed of thatch and wood, or blood and tooth. In the smoulder-stench of the aftermath, one survivor deduced that the peculiar avian occurrence of a fortnight before must have had something to do with this catastrophic fire. *An omen*. Such a suggestion, once spoken aloud, spread quickly, for *Yes*, they said, *Yes, of course* the birds were an omen of the fire to come. They had all seen the two huge populations of starlings that had gathered in the sky that day, hadn't they, screeching their eerie tunes? They had all seen the bird-war that followed too, leaving the city splattered with feathered corpses.

No one had understood it at first, but suddenly the fire made sense, now that it could be rewritten as the repercussion of an omen. The bird-blood that smeared the walls and roofs must have been a warning of the red flames to come. What is an omen if not a translation of the past to fit a new form?

When such omens take flight through our lives, they swoop like echoes. When a human wants to test an echo, they always choose the same word to call.

—

'Hello?'

   'Hello?'

   All morning, a pair of strangers have been flitting from house to house through the village of Boolymore. The door they rap now belongs to a neat little cottage nestled in a neat little garden, where a neat little woman lives alone. This woman is known by three names. To her friends and neighbours, she is either Norrie Singleton or Nora Ní Shindile, but to the two officials who have arrived to inspect her rented property as part of Griffith's Valuation, she gives her name as Honoria Singleton.

   She tugs her shawl around her shoulders, cloaking herself in dark wool punctuated with speckles of ash, and spells her name carefully. *Yes. H-O-N-O-R-I-A. Sir.* The men's eyes soon adjust to the smoky gloom of her cottage, taking in her belongings – the súgán stools, the kettle over the fire, the basketful of turf, the clutch of eggs in their chipped bowl, the thimble next to a spool of dark thread, the dresser, the delph, the silver scissors, the yellow curtains hemmed by her own hand – but these men have not arrived to compile an inventory of an old woman's belongings. Her house is assessed at 5 shillings, and the small patch of land she keeps? Worthless.

Both worthless and priceless, her invisible heirloom, for within her, she holds a vast library of precious antiques. Norrie may have had three different names by which she was variously known, but to all, she was known by her encyclopaedic knowledge of song and story, for the bright slant to her eye and the tilt of her head. People travelled from afar to sit and watch her eyelids drop as she sought the thread with which to begin, and they stayed for hours, listening to her voice, enchanted.

Norrie lived a long and cultured life, her door always ajar to visiting musicians and storytellers. Located about eight hours' walk from the elegance of Raleigh House, it was from this small cottage that Eibhlín Dubh's *Caoineadh* was translated from voice to text for the first time. It was handwritten with care, moving mouth to ear to hand to page, and onwards into English, the language in which it would be published by Mrs O'Connell. We cannot know from whose mouths the echoes of our lives will chime. Norrie is the source and the surface from which Eibhlín Dubh's voice reverberates to us. Little starling: she opens her mouth, and someone else's words chirp out.

—

In my November, the starlings are landing on wires that extend from the city into the west. Neither Norrie nor Eibhlín would have recognised these cables, nor the tall silver pylons that punctuate the places so familiar to them. They would both, however, have known the starlings that perch there, the neat lines in which they cluster, chattering snatches of new sounds mixed with those handed down from long before, passed beak to beak, quick as gossip. From a distance, such birds might appear drab, but to look closely is to see the petrol-blue iridescence of their plumage, how their cloaks are speckled, with stars perhaps – or with ash.

13. to splinter the surface

gur thit ár gcúirt aolda,

our bright-limed home tumbling,

—Eibhlín Dubh Ní Chonaill

THE GESTURE OF PINCHING CLOTHES to the line requires my arms to reach skywards, to where clouds gush by, a flood suspended in layers of silvers and greys. I could be underwater, now; I could be breathing liquid, looking up to a Beyond that exists on the other side of the swell that hovers overhead. Call it a cloud.

—

Deep in an old, old night, our city lies dark in the valley. Behind one draped window, a woman startles awake from a nightmare; even in sleep, her grief cannot still itself. In the dread half-light, she sees her home crumpled to ruin, the lands all shrivelled, the animals vanished, the air deathly silent, 'The Gearagh all withering, / without a growl left of your hounds / nor the sweet chirp of birds'. In her time, The Gearagh was an ancient alluvial forest punctuated with pastures and farms. The landscape itself was birthed long before, when an Ice Age glacier at Gougane Barra disintegrated, releasing a vast body of meltwater. In the gush and squash and crush of that flood, clusters of debris were shoved into hillocks. Grass grew. Weeds. Thorn bushes. Slow, those old centuries, as a forest was born of hawthorn, hazel, oak, and ash, where new birds sang new songs from each new branch. Soon, human voices lilted among those trees too, tending to the first generations of bovine jaws to gurn The Gearagh's cud to milk.

Women worked by bucket-handles there, by brushes, pots and shovels, pinning clothes to lines, tossing grain to birds, feeding calves, hefting bucketfuls of well-water, peeling potatoes, holding children to their breasts, sighing and singing and stirring, and when everyone else slept, they bent in candlelight, darning fraying hems to suspend further unravelments. This was The Gearagh Eibhlín Dubh knew: hectic, boisterous, and invincible. Silence? Here? Impossible. For centuries this place defied her nightmare, in the laughter and song and turf smoke that continued to lilt on the breeze.

The first destruction of The Gearagh occurred in text. In the 1950s, planning documents detailed a hydro-electric scheme, the construction of dams, and a strategic flooding. Hands were raised, documents signed. A man lifted a map and circled an evacuation zone. Others nodded. The carts, the cows, the children, everything was led away, all the belongings and furnishings, the chairs and the tables, the baskets and pots and blankets, all carried to safety. Did the people lock their doors before they left? Did they leave keys in keyholes, or tie them on twine around their necks? In the distance, the river. Each ripple tense as a harp string. Plucked. Trembling.

The brutal heft of liquid comes rude and fast, flinging open doors without knocking, rushing through private rooms, finding any clothing left behind: the torn, the ill-fitting, and the useless. Water smiles, puppeting those limbs, jigging legs and arms until they turn to rags, and then to fragments of rags, dancing them and dancing again until every ragged dress's warp is tugged from its weft. A grand and ordinary unravelment, this, how fast the fabric of a soundscape can be unpicked. For six hours I think about that water as I rewrite these pages on a train, sharing a table with strangers who get drunk and drunker, laugh loud and louder, slamming the melamine table with football-chant fists until the keyboard shudders to my fingertips. *No flinching*. Each time I loop back to rewrite these paragraphs, I must watch The Gearagh flooding again. When I type the word 'puppeting', some invisible clock-hand ticks, some secret key twists, and without noticing, I bleed. Drop follows dark drop. Blot. Blot. Another daughter, dropped. The empty rooms of The Gearagh sing only of liquid. In my pocket is a tissue imprinted with dabbed lipstick, a sequence of wordless mouths come unstuck, each one red as blood.

———

When I visit, the waters are low, allowing ancient stumps to splinter the surface, their bleak limbs pointing, but towards what, I can't tell. I've heard that the old rooftops can sometimes be seen through the water, so I lean my body over those deep gardens, all trembling with waterweed, where fish fly like crows. I am peering down from far above now, and although I don't see them, I do feel them below, the hidden rooms where women fed milk to infants and lambs, where candles were quenched by their weary breaths, where they called their lovers' names in rage, in desire, or in fear, where they roared as new life thundered from them, *Oh god, Oh god, Oh god,* all those hidden rooms in which they smiled and died – they exist still, somewhere beyond the surface, even if no one sees them.

> Knock Knock.
> Who's there?

Back at my own clothesline, I think of those women. I arrange my body as they did: I look up. The clouds seem a flood, suspended far overhead. Our pasts are deep underwater. Our pasts are submerged in elsewheres.

—

Elsewhere, the years were turning Máire's long hair grey, folding all her bright silk gowns into chests, closing the lids and turning the keys. Her frocks were replaced by a subdued costume Mrs O'Connell describes as 'black silk, with white coif and kerchief, and plain cambric ruffles'. Modest, yes, but never less than elegant.

In 1795, Máire died. She was keened by Alice, Eibhlín's sister. Eibhlín would have been in her early fifties if she was present to watch her mother's coffin cradled over the sands towards Abbey Island. There, sharp blades unlocked the deep door through which her husband's body had moved decades before, and into that room of soil, Máire Ní Dhuibh's body was lowered.

Night fell.

Night fell over all the footprints pressed into the strand.

Night fell over the forest and the kitchen garden, over the stables and the mountain.

Night fell over Máire's roof, and night entered her home room by room, embracing all that was left of her life. Dark, her silver; dark, her keys; dark, her mirrors; dark, her cabinets; dark, her sons; dark, her daughters; and beyond their sleeping eyelids, all was dark, dark, dark.

The gravestone arrived much later, with its inscription describing her as 'a model for wives and mothers to admire and imitate'. I smiled the first time I ran my fingers over those stone words, but I do admire her, don't you?

I think again of Eibhlín, alone, her heels galloping her hearthstone. Below lies a mare's skull, and in the orbits where eyes once moved, there is only dark.

—

When Mrs O'Connell visited Derrynane a century after Máire's death, she set to cataloguing all the traces of her life that still resounded through those rooms. She thought Máire's belongings 'exempt from the mutabilities of time and fate'. She thought them invincible; she thought them safe. She was wrong.

By the time I arrive, another hundred years have passed, and not only have all Máire's objects vanished, but the rooms through which she once strode have been erased too. All that remains of the home Eibhlín Dubh was raised in is the series of extensions constructed during her famous nephew Daniel's era, his home having been repurposed as a museum. When his home was first entrusted to the Irish State in the 1960s, Máire's house was intact at the heart of the complex, but it was soon pronounced structurally unsound. Although Daniel's rooms would be allowed to remain, officials decided that the older part of the house would be too expensive to save. The usual administrative routines were set in motion – the hands raised, the documents signed, and then, thud by violent thud, Máire's rooms were obliterated.

I stand within her old borders now, in the breezy gravel among the tourists and tour-guides, and try not to feel embarrassed as I let my eyelids fall. Like a prayer or a spell, I recite to myself the inventory of objects Mrs O'Connell documented here, all those belongings that Máire loved, her quaint old massive silver, the rare and beautiful oriental china, the rococo mirrors she smuggled, dark mahogany furniture she and her husband had made, beautiful brass scutcheons around keyholes, huge china punch bowl, blue and white fruit baskets, long handled silver spoon for stirring jam [that] was already in [its] 6th generation ...

The word *scutcheon* is new to me. My phone explains that in the eighteenth century, it referred both to the ornate metal panel surrounding a keyhole, and also to a marking behind a cow's udder (known as the 'milk mirror', and once thought an indicator of the volume of milk a cow might produce). Máire's brass scutcheons opened only to her keys. If each key of hers could be considered a word, her belted ring would have comprised an extraordinarily rare female text. Where is it?

I let the gravel become a kitchen floor and make the room around me busy with women. I charm the air until it fills itself with steam, gossip, and the smell of warm bread. I let myself untether further until I can almost see beyond the hall and stairs and into another sunlit room. In the old parlour, my palms linger on an imagined windowsill. Within these walls, I have lifted puppet-strings until a breath flickered alive in the fireplace, setting three embers dancing again. I have beckoned dawn through these windows and set footsteps over its floorboards. I have arranged drapes to frame these windows just so, and settled chairs with neatly plumped cushions. I have hung a rococo mirror on the wall to reflect the candles as they were lit in the evenings, doubling their flicker-light.

A mirror like Máire's would have been born in a workshop abroad, in France, perhaps, where twin sheets of coarse glass would have been drawn against each other, separated only by a layer of water and sand, creating a friction that burnished both surfaces until they gleamed. Next, an interior layer of silvering, tin foil, and liquid mercury would have been applied, followed by polishing and bevelling. Born into its frame and bound in soft fabrics, it would have been lifted over depths of salt-rush and agitated sand, over dolphins and basking sharks, moving ever closer to Máire. When finally it was fixed to the wall at Derrynane, she would surely have smiled, seeing her own eyes reflected there for the first time. How precious such a mirror must have been when it first arrived, made so both by its elegance and by its rarity. Such an extravagance quickly became commonplace, however, as time brought mirrors to many other homes, until this object became an unremarkable word in the vocabulary of that room. By demolition, Máire's mirror may have still been present, or it may already have become unfashionable by then, removed in favour of a more chic style. Maybe it had fallen, a splintering omen. If Máire's mirror did smash to the floor of Derrynane, who might have been present to gather the seven years of ill-fortune that followed?

I have sought out such mirrors on antiques websites, charmed by the intricacies of their gilt vines and blossoms. Antiques of this era are now so old that their frames are often displayed alone, their mirror-glass replaced by dark felt, conjuring an abyss where a reflected face would once have been. 'O,' such empty mirrors seem to say,

> O
> O shadow
> O iris
> O lost twin
> O darkness
> O, O, O.

Mirrors speak a language of reflection and refraction through a continually shifting pattern of symmetries. *See-saw, saw-she*: at night, when Máire's mirror dreams, she leaves the fidelity of glass behind and brings back old faces instead. The craftsman who birthed her. The boy who bound her in sacking. The maid with her spiralling cloth. Máire's hum, the silver melody of keys keeping time with her steps: *for-ev-er, for-ev-er*. Mary lifting an apple from a blue-and-white basket.

Nelly pausing to tuck a stray lock back in her braid. This is how the years pass in that mirror: soon, too soon. Someday, it, too, will be absent, and so will the room, but for now, they cling to each other. The mirror holds the dark room, and the room holds the dark mirror.

—

Beyond the gravel, a clutch of tourists are strolling between the gift shop and tea-rooms, plump as toddlers. I wish I could enjoy the pleasures of Derrynane as they seem to, but I can't think of anything beyond Eibhlín Dubh. I recently received news that a book of mine, with a poem inspired by her life, has been given a literary award generous enough to help us put a down-payment on a house of our own. I can't help but feel that Eibhlín Dubh had a hand in this achievement, and yet, I am so focused on finding her that I can't celebrate. I envy these tourists their serenity, so I mimic them; I feign a smile like theirs and follow them through the museum, past the displays devoted to Daniel O'Connell, his plaques and his golden carriage, his many leather-bound books, even his death-bed, all immaculately preserved. *A great man. O, a great man.*

I find a guide and ask after Máire, and then her daughters, to a nodding smile and the word 'minor'.

I start to scowl but catch myself and ask after older artefacts instead: the mirrors, the china, and the scutcheons. When I ask after keys for doors that no longer exist, the guide's smile falters at one corner, and once I begin to describe a particularly old jam spoon, the smile finally falls, and I am alone. I scour every one of those immaculate rooms for any remnant of the women I seek – a single button, say, a nib, a candlestick, or an earring – any trace at all of their existences. I find nothing.

The last tourist bus leaves and the house quietens, letting each of the rooms settle once more into the particularity of its own silence. On the staircase, I dawdle, disheartened, my head leaning against the wall that once bordered the old house. I am tired. I knock – *soft, soft* – but where my knuckling might once have moved an echo through rooms on the other side, now, there is nothing. I should be on the road towards home already, I think, fumbling for my phone to check the time. From behind, a blare of sunlight leaps from the clouds, drawing my shadow on the wall, ink-black and inarticulate, a female body sketched by light. The clarity of this sudden reflection shakes me, and I stumble back, grasping for the balustrade. The shape dulls, then melts, fleeting and female, just as their shadows were. I continue to stare at the wall, willing it to return, longing to translate what it might mean, until I sense someone watching. From the foot of the stairs, the guide is peering up at me with something like sympathy. She must think me unstable, I realise, and she wouldn't be wrong – what I consider an epiphany is simply my own shadow. I smile, shaking my head, as I thank her and thank her again. Hurrying away, I am still smiling to myself.

My heels sing me from gravel to paving stones, into wet leaves, and then onto sparser winter grass. Another November-chill night is inching up from the ocean as my gaze rakes the ground, picking a cautious path through its slick murk. I don't want to fall. From that dirt, something winks. Something pale and pointed. I kneel and scrape it up by fingernail. To my elation, I find that it is a fragment of delph, painted with a sliver of some delicate flower, a fragment of an old bowl, perhaps, a saucer or a teacup. It grins at me; I grin back. This was once part of a vessel from which steam rose to air, dissipated, then disappeared, a vessel that was often rubbed under warm suds until the day it slid from human grip to smash with a curse, this vessel whose fragments were quickly scooped up, slid into a bin, and flung on a rubbish heap. There, its splinters were cloaked in mud and rotting peelings, dispersed by years and by worms, through growth and frost and sun and snow, until this moment, when finally it chose to lift its face, giving itself to female hands once more. Little treasure. I rub it between my fingers and it grows warm. I translate it into a sign. Whether or not this fragment could be traced to Máire's or Nelly's hand doesn't bother me. All that matters is that I am lifting an artefact symbolic of the female lives and thought and labour that belonged to this place. I hold this chunk in the heart of my hand, as gently as I hold every fragment I have found of Eibhlín Dubh's life. Even in the half-light, it shines. I try to imagine extrapolating a whole from it, unbroken and vivid. Máire's belongings may have disappeared, but in the island soil her teeth still grin, pearl-pale.

—

I have taken, of late, to seeking out flesh on the internet, opening incognito windows to swipe endless placentae in wonder and revulsion, in squirm and in awe. I scroll through them, so labyrinthine, so meaty, and wonder how my own flaws might have looked. This compulsive searching leads me to an article from the Smithsonian Institute on microchimerism. In pregnancy, I read, pluripotent cells from the foetus move through the placenta and enter the mother's bloodstream. Within her body, they cling to tissues, mimicking the composition of surrounding cells, and there, they remain, long after the baby has left. A collection of such cells from subsequent siblings may be all stored within the mother simultaneously, each cluster coordinating and conflicting with a mother's own bodily impulses. I think of Máire Ní Dhuibh, alone on the strand, her eye on the horizon, as her twin infants swim the ocean inside her. Even after both had grown and gone, she may have returned there, thinking of her daughters, far away in their own lives. Just as they remained in her thoughts, some of their cellular matter also remained in her body, vestigial, lingering.

In her *Caoineadh*, although Eibhlín Dubh curses Mary's husband and their children, she can't bring herself to wish any ill on her twin –

> Only let no harm fall on Mary,
> and not for much sisterly love,
> but only that my own mother
> made her a first bed within her,
> where we shared three seasons together.

Eibhlín respected that red room still, the shared womb in which their twin placentas grew close, and so, she sheltered Mary from her curse. We presume to know so little of what occurs beyond or within us, whether of the lived past or of our unseen cellular mechanisms, and yet, at some level, we do instinctively understand something of these mysteries. Even as her twins raged at each other, fossils of their cells persisted within their mother's body. Máire still held them both close.

—

I don't push the fragment of delph back into its anonymous garden grave. I hold it tight, just as I hold every shard of information I've learned of Eibhlín Dubh. I close my fingers around it and run. I steal it.

My car mirror is the only eye that recognises my thievery. As I drive, I think of Máire and her daughters' reflected eyes, and I think of their lost mirror, but in my own, whose face do I see? Only me, only me. I can't bear it.

Swivelling it away, I catch the glare of the wet road instead, silver and grey as an unravelling braid. A convex seer, this rear-view mirror lets me peer into the landscape unwinding behind me, but it cannot show what is ahead, nor how I should turn next.

14. now, then

nó thairis dá dtaitneadh liom.

... or beyond
if I'd want.

—Eibhlín Dubh Ní Chonaill

NOW

For two-and-a-half years, the days and nights I have shared with my daughter all brim with milk. I have held her to my breast in airports and supermarkets, on beaches and buses, on footpaths and benches. I have fed her through waking and sleeping, through her fevers, teething, and tummy bugs, and through my own exhaustion, breast infections, mastitis fevers, and jammed ducts. She feeds. I feed. She sleeps. I ache.

Even in my weariest moments, though, there remains a sort of merriness in feeling so useful. My right breast knows her needs intimately and fills them immediately. My left breast, however, still won't work: lazy, brazen lump. From the moment that the skin of my girl-chest began to rise, the left nipple was inverted. Sullen, it never sang to a lover's touch. Whereas my right breast is plump and industrious, the left dozes limply; milk has made of me a lopsided factory.

In the bra-fitting rooms, a stranger shucks her tongue at my body. My right breast requires the substantial architecture of an E cup, the left a small B, a conundrum that represents an impossible arithmetic for any engineer of lingerie. I end up in what a younger version of myself might have mocked as a *granny bra*, unembellished white fabric stitched to tough, sturdy straps, adjusted until one breast is hoisted high while the other lolls in its voluminous cotton pocket. I take to wearing cardigans.

For years, my sleep is broken by milk. Occasionally, as I'm tugged awake, I take comfort in imagining how often this precise moment has been enacted not only by my own body, but by other mothers, again and again and again, each a mirroring of the same elements – *the milk, the mother, the baby, the dark, the milk, the mother, the baby, the dark, the milk, the milk, the milk* – and in such moments, I am excruciatingly tired, yes, and yet, contentment hovers here too, shimmering in the peripheries, regardless of how tired I am. I *am* excruciatingly tired, yes, so tired that

I frequently repeat myself, so very, very tired – and yet, I still procrastinate over whether to wean. To lure this child away from my body and train her hungers elsewhere would be to pull myself from my comfortable burrow of service. I can't do it, the ritual of giving of myself to another is so exquisite. I have made an invisibility of myself, neatly concealed in rooms made by female labour and repetition and milk.

THEN

As a girl, I thought I knew homemaking. By July, the gaps in the old stone walls around our house were bursting with weeds and wild strawberries, the grasses all beginnings, stretching tall and taller by the day. I was ten and free from school. I could feel the end of my childish amusements looming, but this summer, I told myself, I would delight in the joys of girlhood. I kicked off my boots and walked barefoot.

Every summer, I had made myself a place of privacy in the grass, a nest where I could not be seen. My method was always the same – I chose a dip with care, then threw myself to my knees and gave my body to the land. I rolled with all my strength, spine to soil, belly to sky, then umbilical down and back to cloud, flinging myself side to side until I saw only sky and dirt and dirt and sky. I pressed my body into that place until it yielded to me, until I could feel the grass and weeds surrender and release all their seeds to the breeze, until I'd made a hollow that would be mine and mine alone. Call it a home. I pushed myself up on my elbows to admire my ceiling, where clutches of bumblebees stumbled by. The walls swayed. I made an invisibility of myself there, neatly concealed in a room made by female labour and repetition, an echo-imprint of my small existence. It felt like it belonged to me, that hollow, it felt new, and yet, as my body pressed into that ground, it also felt very old. There were others there too, unseen but present all around me.

The days in our home-place had always been the same: the same joys and drudgeries, the same cycles of childbearing and wakes, the same ringforts, the same fields filling and emptying and filling again with voices, with grass, with beasts, and with hay. Everything repeated and repeated again. My family had lived within these hills for centuries. I knew that there had been many other girls who had made their homes on this ground before me, girls who were grown now and gone into the ground themselves, their babies – my great-grandmothers – grown and gone the same way. Nothing I knew was ever truly new; every path I followed had been written by the bodies of others, the course of every track sculpted by the footfall of those who came before us. *For-ev-er. For-ev-er.* To the well. To the haggart. To the shed. To the hill. Along these ways, grasses hummed their old tunes, blackthorns pointed their warnings, and every well held the memory of whispered human desire. Maybe I was a strange child, feeling the constant hum of the past just beyond me, real as a bee, or maybe every child shares that feeling. All I knew was that I felt safe, there, in the echo of their company.

NOW

Weaning. Weaning. My family asks about it often, their brows lifting at the sight of a toddler strutting across the room to tug at my breast. My husband asks too; his sleep is fitful, disturbed and, like me, he is weary. Still, my instincts scold me to tolerate my petty exhaustion and focus instead on giving my daughter all she needs – she takes such comfort from her moments of milk that to deprive her of it seems not only selfish, but somehow cruel. I find that I'm too tired to keep going, but too tired to summon the determination to wean. What should I do? If I sought advice from my past – if I called a question of my body – what reply might I receive?

Eventually, my body makes the decision on my behalf. *No more*, my exhaustion says, *no more*. First to go is my daughter's dawn feed, our beloved morning ritual snuggled under the duvet, her head in my elbow. One morning, she wakes to a voice calling her from downstairs instead. Before she can roar for milk, she is already splattering her spoon in a bowl of porridge and fruit. The following week, I begin the slow reduction of her many afternoon feeds. Whenever she tugs at my sleeve, I pass her a sippy-cup of water instead. Sometimes she glugs it happily, eyes grinning beyond the neon tilt of plastic. Other days she slaps it out of my hand, screeching in outrage and grief, throwing herself to the ground and flinging herself side to side. *Mama*, she screeches, *Give. Me. NUMNUMS*. Fat tears roll down her cheeks as she beats the floor with her fists. The part of me well-trained in subduing my own desires observes such displays in admiration. I stroke her hair and tell her the old lie, 'Hush, now, hush, everything will be OK.' She soon grows used to the new shape of her days, stirring only once at night for water. She sleeps, now. I sleep too.

Ten years have passed in which I have been pregnant, or breastfeeding, or both. Quietly, I hope that there will be another baby to busy me soon, but now, for the first time in a decade, I dream through the night, undisturbed. My sleeping mind leads me to a house on a hill, where milk is rippling every window. Peering in, I see that pale liquid pouring thickly over every bed and chair, over floorboards and rafters, jostling every kettle, TV, and laundry basket, every radio and phone, in tides of deep, dense milk. My dreaming knuckle raps the door. *Knock knock.* A woman is sweeping through those sunken rooms, her broom glimpsed, then gone, then glimpsed again, dark hair floating tall over her head, eyes on the floor. She can't see me. I knock again. *Who's there?* she says, smiling to herself, and when her neck twists, her eyes are full and white, staring with milk. I wake, shaking. What will become of me, in the absence of this labour, all this growing and harvesting? Without milk, how will I see? Without milk, who will I be?

THEN

My childhood home stood on a steep hill whose precarious angles refused the press of balers and other modern machinery. Once the grass stretched elbow-high, my father rumbled up in an old tractor. Inside, my mother worried that the slope would defeat him, sending his vessel toppling. It didn't. The field was soon translated into stubble, sharp underfoot. I tugged on my wellies and gathered armfuls of hay while my father pitchforked neat stacks. The sun did her duty well: she worked every blade of grass until it dried to a brittle filament and they could all be hefted to the shed. Colossus: that wall of hay reached right to the roof. It seemed so strange, how this displaced volume of grasses could fill a room with enough fuel to nurture others' hunger through the cold months to come. Outside, it had been conquerable even by a girl like me, but in here, it was immense. Even indoors, though, my body remembered the grass. I wondered if it remembered me too.

NOW

Once I stop breastfeeding, my right breast shrinks fast. It sags, exhausted and stretch-marked, making the lazy breast the plumper of the two. After a shower, I finally meet my own gaze in the mirror I have so often polished unseeingly, observing the purplish smudges that shadow each of my eyes. I drop the towel, and document my body with curiosity: my milk-bottle thighs split by turquoise seams; my breasts, lopsided and glorious; the holy door of my quadruple caesarean scar, my sag-stomach, stretch-marked with ripples like a strand at low tide. My bellybutton grimaces there, the invisible cord that will always connect me to my mother, just as hers connects her to her mother, and on, and on, and on. I study this body of mine, just one more in a long line, and feel no revulsion, only pride. *This is a female text*, I think. My body replies in its dialect of scars. *Ta-dah!* it seems to say, *Ta-dah!*

—

My right breast continues to dwindle as it cleans itself of residual milk-clutter. I throw all my old nursing bras into the bin, goodbying their grey cotton cups and their well-worn plastic clips. Finished – *tick*. Somewhere in the warm dark of my body, another clock was tick-ticking, building something that will soon threaten me, but I don't know that yet.

My new bra comes home swaddled in layers of frothy pink tissue and ribbon. To tug its clips into place is to lift my breasts to a false illusion of perkiness. In this elaborate edifice of metal and lace, my breasts appear almost normal, as though I'd never used them at all – but the body remembers. When I squeeze my right nipple, a pale drop winks back.

THEN

By autumn, stiff new school shoes were scrambling me all the way to the top of the hay mountain. I was in trouble again. I stretched myself in my high nest and pouted. I had been lazy, and now my mother was angry, dangling a plastic bracelet she'd found in my pocket. Such carelessness could have destroyed the washing machine, and then what would she do? I was a brazen child, I shrugged at her scowl and sprinted away before she could catch me.

High in the hay, I'd hidden a bag that held some glucose barley pastilles and a comic, and now I tucked myself so close to the rafter that I could see every rough splinter. When those old-fashioned pastilles were sucked sharp, they sliced my gums, and a red tang slid through the sweetness. Somewhere in the warm dark of my body, a clock was tick-ticking. I pinched my eyes tight and tighter until the dark behind my eyelids exploded like fireworks, and made myself a little bat, tucked snug all day, dreaming herself back into night. My mother's voice soared the air, and in my hurry down before my hidden room was discovered, I found myself slipping face first, the force too quick for me to grip any of the hay's slipping blades, until I landed on the shit-dark floor of the shed, my mouth smashing into the steel of a gas barrel. I sat up and spat half a front tooth into my palm. It was pale and wet and red, all at once. My mother screamed.

'Don't you worry,' the dentist said, eyes smiling above his mask, 'we'll have you back to yourself in no time. Now then, deep breath for the needle – good girl.' He built a careful symmetry in my mouth, binding a fragment of the past to a new present. In the mirror, the tooth looked so real, an intermingling of truth and fiction visible every time I spoke. My precious artifice: where my tooth is bound to the prosthetic, my mouth holds both truth and lie.

NOW

Every day, I kneel in the same pew and pray to the same god as my mother, with its halo of detergent and its holy whirr. I repeat her devotion, rummaging my children's pockets for perils lurking beyond the rustle of fabric: a coin or a pine cone, a marble or a conker. One night, I find a hard little bump tucked into the pocket of my left breast. My fingers stop, then fumble back. Snuggled in layers of breast tissue, I find a second one. A second what? My mind screams one word, *over* and *over* again.

Again, I feel myself slipping. I try to talk myself out of panicking, telling myself that such lumps might be some sort of side-effect of lactation, but in truth, I know that's impossible. This is my left breast after all, it hasn't produced more than a drop of milk in years. Besides, I am intimately familiar with every permutation of mastitis: the shivering fever, the weakness, the horror, the swelling infection. This is different. What if I hadn't weaned my daughter, I think, might I have prevented this?

On the morning that a doctor's hand hunts my breast for further clues, my eye flies through the window, carrying me elsewhere. He is an exceptionally kind man, warm and caring, but his hands today are cold. Once he finds the second lump, his voice calls me back from the distance. He is frowning at my left nipple, inverted and shy. I think of the many occasions when this man has heard me imagine a baby's heat-rash into meningitis, or worrying a bump into a fractured skull, and I will him with all my might to grin again now. Instead, he pokes my armpit, then squeezes my breast again. I hear my voice quiver like a child's, and when words emerge, they too, are the words of a child. '... but – but, will everything be OK?' He prints a letter referring me onwards for further tests. 'We just need some more information, that's all. Go home, have a cup of tea. Try not to worry.' When I slide five crumpled tenners towards the receptionist, my face remembers its script and twists itself into a polite smile. That's all.

In the car park, the steering wheel cradles my brow as tears puddle my lap, each drawing its own slow, salty pool in the fabric. Beyond, three skinny starlings grip a wire in silence. I look to the rooftops, where satellite dishes turn their ears skywards, straining to catch invisible signals from the dark distance. I know, then, where I need to be. I don't go home; I turn the key.

At Kilcrea, the silver stones of the door welcome me back in their cold way. I tell myself that I don't know why I've come here, but I do. I do. I don't recall which words I utter, I only know that my face grows wet and my throat grows hoarse. I take comfort in the knowledge that I am far from the first woman to have wept in this place, where I am both surrounded by others, and utterly, utterly alone.

THEN

Alone, I was shivering on the toilet, my breath a cloud between me and a word I'd never seen before, a streak scrawled by my child-body on a wad of paper. Pale and wet and red all at once, the sight made me wonder whether my tooth in its palmful of blood had been an omen of sorts. I wasn't sure how to translate this text, but I knew it meant change and I knew it meant shame. It would have to be concealed. This was how my body turned towards womanhood – in reluctance and in fear. I wished I could resist this change somehow, that I could choose, instead, to stay in my days of girlish invisibility. I folded a book of clean tissue and tucked it against my skin. I'd have to make myself read it later, and if it held more words by then, I'd probably have to tell my mother. How I hoped those pages would remain unwritten. The following week, I was chewing gum when a man said I looked like a *slut*. I wasn't entirely sure how to translate that word either, but by the way he spat it I deduced that it couldn't be good. At home, I unwrapped more gum, but all the mirror saw in me was a shy little animal grinding her cud.

NOW

At the breast clinic, I am one of nine women sitting topless under identical dressing gowns. Abrasive and dense, the fabric rubs horribly against the skin. I hate these garments, and I hate this room. From the wall, the usual saints grimace, their haloes a perfect match for their yellow plastic frames. The TV chats incessantly as Judge Judy reprimands a line of people who have misbehaved, pointing at them in ferocity until they wince like dogs, hands stretched to her in supplication, with their wounded feelings, and their hurt paws. Bored, I walk to the window.

My view of the city is peculiar from this height, a map of all the roads I got lost in as a student, suddenly coherent from this new distance. My gaze soars the rooftops of college flats, prefabs, and the ornate gables of Victorian three-stories, until I find the long, modest roof of the Colletine Monastery. In its snug attic, bats are sleeping. Pipistrelles. It is the largest colony in the city, or so I have heard. Soon, the females will form their seasonal mothering clusters, and then, by milk and by warmth, their infants will grow, until autumn finds them weaned and ready to leap from the attic into dark lives of their own.

Two decades before, when I should have been at anatomy class, I sat in that chapel alone, viciously hungover, staring upwards through the stained glass. I didn't know about the bats then, but they were present nevertheless, cloaked and dreaming somewhere beyond my broken silhouette. I knelt. I wept. More than anything, I wanted to die. Now I find myself peering down at that same glass from a window high on the other side, longing to live. My phone rings but when I fumble it from my bag and answer, no one is there. *Hello?* I say. *Hello?* I wait for an answer. None comes.

A nurse calls my name, and I follow her smile to a new room. I wish I could resist the change in my body somehow, that I could remain happily unseen in my days of domestic invisibility. An hour later I am leaving the hospital, fumbling plastic headphones into my ears. In a room behind me, I am leaving a biopsy of my flesh. I may appear unremarkable to any pedestrian I pass, but under my summer dress, under layers of bandage and gauze, under fifteen syringe holes, a large hematoma is weeping blood into the darkness. A deep bruise is gathering there, swift as a cloud-shadow over The Gearagh.

THEN

The shed grew colder as the hay left, blade by blade ground out of existence by the slow slide of spittle and tooth. Each bolus of cud was rollercoasted through multiple stomachs and then shat back to ground in extravagant splats. In its aftermath was a newly resonating emptiness that seemed the antithesis of my once-cosy home. To test its acoustics I rocked back and forth in my boots, toe to heel, heel to toe, shouting to myself: *Hello? Hello?* and smiling at the aural chime my voice provoked from the walls. The rafters seemed impossibly distant already. I knew

I would never reach them again. Now only bats would know that splintered closeness.

NOW

I wait for biopsy results. I fret. I wait. I fret.

The letter comes wrapped in an envelope of inarticulable relief, followed quickly by confusion. That no cancerous cells have been detected is the only answer the tests provide; they hazard no explanation for the lumps. Soon, more letters arrive for more appointments, more tests, more waiting under the sharp fingers of Judge Judy.

The surgeon's tie is a soft pendulum as he kneads my breast, his head tilting a question mark. His verdict is that although the lumps are inexplicable, they are not cancerous, so his scalpel need not touch my skin. My fists open in relief. Somewhere nearby, a bat stirs in her sleep.

Just as I resisted its red scrawl, I have longed to resist this truth of my body, but now I try to accept its strangeness. In my left breast I carry two lumps, neat as ammonite fossils, each a clue. When my body lies in a dissection room, a student may read these texts as easily as they will read my tattoo, my caesarean scar, or my broken tooth, translating them into the gallons I set ricocheting through the bodies of others. I think of them as commas, although they feel more like full stops. My days of milk are beginning to seem impossibly distant, as though I may never reach them again, as though only others will know that splintered closeness. It cannot be. No matter what unfolds, I tell myself that I will always hold my souvenir: the pearl and the pebble of an inner brooch fixed firmly within my chest. Whether it is a glitch or an embellishment, this is a female text, and I carry it close to my heart.

15. a sequence
of shadows

ONCE EIBHLÍN DUBH'S name ceases to appear in her brothers' letters, my letters, too, falter on the screen. My sources, I fear, have dwindled to their ends. The bolted entrance of Raleigh House cannot admit me, nor can the demolished rooms of old Derrynane. All the objects I long to see have been either erased or concealed, every brooch gone, every cup dropped, every door locked, every key lost. There's no evidence left of her life, nothing left to find. And yet. And yet, I can't accept it. There is still so much we don't know. We don't know how long she lived, whether she reconciled with her family, whether she married again, whether she had further children or stepchildren. We don't know where she lived out her remaining years, or how she sustained herself financially. Although the gravestone at Kilcrea identifies where her husband, son and grandson are all buried, the location of Eibhlín Dubh's bones was never noted. One moment, we hear her voice, real and distinct, and the next, *Ta-dah!*, quick as an illusionist, she disappears.

I try to teach myself to adapt to this sudden absence, just as I have been learning to accept another absence in my days. While I have been dwelling on the many mysteries of Eibhlín Dubh's life, my daughter has been growing. She has her own little satchel now, to carry on her own little back. Every morning, I hold her hand and wave her goodbye at playschool, watching her hurry towards the paint-pots and jigsaws and dress-up box. I spend the subsequent hours scraping uselessly at the same old archival sources. Eibhlín Dubh is never there. My mornings are too quiet, now that my children, my purpose, and my ghost have all left me. I count the minutes until I can lift my daughter into my arms again, a squirming, living female text. At night, I cuddle her to sleep and think of Eibhlín Dubh stroking her sons' warm hair until their eyelids flicker in dream. I imagine her lifting her head and with one last sigh, the candle is quenched. To darkness. This is it: *The End*.

It can't be.

I keep straining to peer through that dark, attempting to see her nocturnal tableau as something other than an ending. I grow frantic, seeking some new line of enquiry, anything that might allow me to continue this journey. If I can't follow their mother, then what about her children? Perhaps an echo of her life might be traced as it moved through the bodies of those she set in motion. To map their lives might reveal some glimpse of their mother – a letter in which they mention her, maybe, a ledger entry, or a record of her gravestone – something, I think. Anything.

This shift allows me a new path with new clues. At the playschool, I kiss my daughter, and before the door even closes between us, my body is already turning away. For every minute of the following hours I am searching archives, graveyard inscriptions, and old church ledgers of births, marriages, and deaths, building my own jumbled genealogy of Eibhlín Dubh's family. At first, I can't quite see them, these people she knew – they are a sequence of shadows, opaque and distant – but as the weeks pass, the file I build on each name starts to grow. One by one, her people step from gloom to light and walk towards me. They begin to move and to breathe – sometimes flawed and affable, sometimes strange, sometimes violent or irate – these people who knew Eibhlín Dubh. They are real and true. They are.

—

My search for Eibhlín and Art's eldest son is blessed from the outset by concrete clues. Because he is buried with his father in Kilcrea Abbey, their shared gravestone allows me a reliable framework of dates to begin from, dates that let me stroll straight into the yellowed parchments of archive pages and old newspapers, until I begin to find ripples of his life moving through text. I compile a long list of facts and quotes, and then, as is my wont, I daydream it to life.

Eibhlín Dubh was twenty-five years old when she bent over her belly and let out a sharp cry. For hours, she crumpled and crawled and roared until finally, her first baby, a boy, was born. Before he even had a name, he lay in his mother's arms in a bedroom of Raleigh House, where, on the threshold of autumn, she held his body in hers, folded within her arms, and hummed the songs of her girlhood. The light grew golden as she searched for her people in the squished mirror of his face, but found only Art's reflection. The baby's name held his father's family too, for it was shared by both his grandfather and his young uncle: *Conchubhar*, which would be anglicised as Cornelius. This baby grew strong in the warmth of his grandparents' home, where his first gurgles were greeted with shared delight, where he was lifted by his mother from room to room, kissed and sung to, swaddled and carried through the cobbled courtyard over which an eagle watched.

Conchubhar grew. He began to tilt his head and peer around him, seeing flowers, a horse, golden leaves giving themselves to the breeze. One morning, he lifted his arms to his mother and smiled a toothless grin. He began to eat, soft carrot goo rolling down his chin. A tooth pierced his gum. Then, another. I give him the first word spoken by every baby I have known: *Da-Da*. He crawled, moving fast by knee and arm, while Eibhlín Dubh hovered over him. An old chair held his hand as he tugged himself to stand. He took a step. Two. He began to run. Every so often, Conchubhar's father came home. The boy was surely held in Art's arms for a trot across the meadow, squealing with glee as butterflies and bees hurried up from those long grasses. He was still little when his mother's belly began to grow again, and soon, the rooms of Raleigh filled with the sailing cry of a new brother, Fear, a name which, called aloud, sounds like distance: *Far*. When their father lay dying in the dandelions of Carriganima, Conchubhar was three, and his brother was still a baby. No matter how he wept, nothing could change; his daddy was gone, and his mother would never be the same again.

After the *Caoineadh*, Conchubhar disappears, hand-in-hand with his little brother. I find no trace of either child for years, nothing of their tree-climbing, nothing of their learning to write or read or ride, nothing of their pranks or birthdays, of falls or games or fights. All I can glean of the second son is that his name was anglicised as Ferdinand O'Leary, and that he became a priest, although there is no evidence of this in any of the clergy's records – unsurprising, I presume, given how clandestine the practice of Catholicism was in that era. I search until my eyes ache from the jolting scroll of microfilm, and still, I cannot pinpoint even the most basic of details of this younger son's life. I find no burial place. I can't even ascertain his exact birthdate, although I hunt through every text I can think of, to no avail. Like his mother, Ferdinand disappears from my grasp completely. Eventually, I bid him goodbye, and turn back to his brother.

By the time we next encounter Conchubhar, I see him tall and strong, with an easy smile. At twenty-one, he strides through the letters that fly between his uncles, the continual back-and-forthing of affection and gossip, of debts and settlements. On 17 April 1789, Eibhlín's brother Daniel writes to Derrynane from Paris: 'I sent you three days agone the receipts of Con O'Leary.' This brief mention is sufficient to let me envision the young Con strolling the grimy laneways and avenues of Paris, just as the city is sparking towards revolution. Might his mother have visited him there, travelling to Paris by sea and by carriage to kiss her son's cheek? Eibhlín Dubh, now in her mid-forties, must have endured a certain amount of intrigue to negotiate a situation whereby her brothers would pay her son's educational expenses. I close my eyes to see.

The cup was too full. She hadn't let herself realise how uneasy she was until she found herself back in this room – same mirror, same drapes, same floorboards – summoning her courage once more. The tea rippled, giving itself over the lip. Drip drip. She sipped the scalding liquid, and rehearsed once more her little speech. She would make herself humble, even slope her shoulders to appear slightly pathetic, if it would help. He would hardly notice the money it would take to send Con to school along with his cousins. She must make him see that this gesture would be no gift to her; she must show that she would continue to suffer. Catching her face in the mirror, she tried to arrange her features in humility. Eyes down. No flinching. The steps drew closer. The door opened. Maurice looked stern, with his mouth drawn at the corners and grey fuzz creeping his collar. She saw a flash of him as a boy, stuck in a tree and bleating for help, and tried to quench her smirk. 'Well?' He spoke gruffly, as though she were a stranger begging a coin on market day. She bit back the curse that burbled up, and prepared instead to grasp his hands in hers. But her arm was as angry as she was. It misjudged the distance from cup to table, breaking the vessel from its handle, sending a glorious ocean of tea all smash and splash over the floor, on which a fury of fragments lifted like shipwrecks. Eibhlín stared at the liquid. Her brother stared at her. It was an accident, but she knew it would not be seen as such; she could either wait to be chastised, or she could speak first. A shimmer of steam rose, giving itself away so easily to air. Before he even opened his mouth, her legs were already striding her into the hall, through the kitchen with its platters of meat and broth on the boil, and out towards the stables. Let Daniel talk sense into him, she thought, and if he wouldn't listen, damn him, she would find some other way to provide for her son. Hurrying through the kitchen garden, she found that a chunk of the cup handle was still in her fist, slicing red through her fingertip. She flung it into a mound of kitchen rubbish as she passed, among the gristle and rot. Walking away, she held the wound to her mouth and scowled.

—

Somehow, Eibhlín Dubh succeeded in engineering a French education for Con. Afterwards, he followed his uncle Daniel into the military as a member of the *Gardes Françaises*, where, according to his gravestone, he became a captain. The letter in which Daniel mentions Con's 'receipts' was written only months before the storming of the Bastille, but we do not know anything of Con's experiences during the chaos that followed. In what is now the *Place de la Concorde*, a guillotine would soon appear. There, a queen would kneel while crowds jeered at the blade, held over her body for one trembling moment. At Raleigh, a crow swoops over the courtyard and lands next to her mother's gift.

From Paris, Con fades back into the shadows, and for some time, I lose him. During these mystery years, he meets Miss Rebecca Gentleman, who is sometimes noted as his first wife. As I can't find any record of this union, I can't bring myself to join in this assumption, although I do mull over how Eibhlín Dubh might have felt attending the wedding of her eldest son, and how she might have behaved as a mother-in-law. I can almost see Rebecca's hair, coiled, twisted and neatly pinned, but I can't quite see her face. I search and search for her through every census and baptismal record of England and Ireland, but Rebecca is unfindable. Again, I fail. Again, I look back to Con.

By the winter of 1805, he has left Paris behind. In his thirties, I find him shivering among a list of entrants to Gray's Inn, an institution in London that monitored admission to the Bar. A cluster of stone buildings huddles around a pair of scenic squares, and there we see him, our Con, strolling to his next class. I prop an armful of books in his elbow and a light drizzle over his shoulders. The rain falls faster and his gait accelerates, ducking him into a doorway to shake drops from his sleeves.

To run a finger over the names of Con's fellow students and say them aloud is almost to see these sons of the elegant homes of Surrey, Devon, and Berkshire, in their expensive overcoats and hats: *Gilbert Hele Chilcott, Robert Phipps, Charles Hodges Ware*. Con was registered among them on 21 November:

> *Cornelius O'Leary, aged 36, eldest son of Arthur O',*
> *late of Raleigh, Co. Cork, gent., deceased.*

We might imagine him strolling back to his own quarters, tired and fumbling for a lucifer match, then striking it roughly to light a candle-wick. We might see him slopping porridge in a gloomy bowl, or tugging on his boots again to stride the smoky streets of

London, hopping puddles and nodding at acquaintances. Did a letter sometimes arrive bearing his name, written in the hand of his mother? How long might such an item rest among a young man's belongings before being cast into a waste bin?

By September 1813, many people, including Con and his cousin, the politician Daniel O'Connell, were agitating successfully against the political brutalities being inflicted in Ireland. An article on the front page of London's *The Morning Chronicle* places Eibhlín Dubh's son in The Bush Tavern for a meeting of Cork Catholic Board 'with Cornelius O'Leary, Esq., in the Chair'. The following year, his name appeared in very different text, the ledger of Marriage Licence Bonds. There, neat slanted loops pressed the letters of Con's name next to another: Mary Purcell. Mary was one of ten children born into a prosperous and long-established Protestant family in Cork. I search old newspapers until I find their official wedding announcement in *The Freeman's Journal* of 4 May 1814 – 'On Monday last, in Cork, Cornelius O'Leary, Esq., Barrister-at-Law, to Mary, only daughter of Goodwin Purcell Esq., late of Kanturk, in that county.' I calculate that Mary was forty and Cornelius forty-six when they walked down the aisle. If Eibhlín Dubh was alive to catch her son's eye as he left the church, she would have been seventy-one.

The newlyweds settled in Cork city, and on 6 October 1815, Cornelius Ferdinand Purcell O'Leary – Eibhlín Dubh's first grandson – was born. This child was ten months old when Mary found herself pregnant again, and on 19 March 1817, Goodwin Richard Purcell O'Leary was born, named after Mary's father and brother. Mary, like Eibhlín Dubh, had given birth to two boys in three years. I find a reference to a third son, Arthur, who died in infancy, and although I have not been able to find an official record of this birth, it is distressing to imagine this family weeping over the loss of another Art.

In September 1998, during a talk in the village of Inchigeelagh to a family gathering of his fellow O'Learys, Peter O'Leary traced Art's genealogy, noting that: 'It is a curious fact that when Cornelius wrote a short account of his life in a family bible at Manch House, he failed to mention his first wife Rebecca, or his third son Arthur. The account was written in Paris in October 1827.' The mention of this Bible intrigues me, but by the time I find his words, the man who spoke them has sadly passed away, and I can find neither a reference to his source, nor any clue to this mysterious Bible's current location. I am hungry for the details I imagine Con must have written there about his mother's life. At a minimum, it would surely provide me with her date of death and place of burial, and as such, it begins to seem like a golden skeleton key: if I could only find this Bible, I could unlock any number of doors. In searching for its location through the archives of its most recent owners – the Conners of Manch – I read many, many unrelated articles, all of them dead ends. In one, published by Edward MacLysaght in 1946, I'm struck by the following line: 'Colonel Conner and his brother, Henry Conner, DJ, both informed me that a considerable quantity of the family papers, including several interesting eighteenth-century diaries, had been destroyed by certain ladies of the family a generation ago.' For such unnamed women to take a family's story and rewrite it by flame – this is a female text.

Con and Mary soon moved away from the city and made their home at Dromore House, a large home among rolling fields closer to Mary's family. I find him in newsprint again in an issue of *The Freeman's Journal* dated Friday, 9 April 1824, when three men were indicted to Cork County assizes for felling and removing his trees. The following year, he appears once more in the letters collated by Mrs O'Connell, having sought a *bourse*, or scholarship, which would enable his eldest son, Cornelius Junior, to study in Paris. His uncles, Maurice and Daniel, hold conflicting views on who should benefit from this opportunity. Daniel writes that:

O'Leary is very desirous to obtain for his eldest Boy the first bourse that falls vacant on the O'Connell foundation in Paris, and surely he has a fair claim to it, yet Maurice, Connor tells me that you and your Brothers have nominated a younger Brother of his to the first vacancy. I must observe to you that you ought never, nay, that you have no right to do so, and that it would be exceedingly unfair to dispose of two Bourses in the same family, to the prejudice of a nearer relation. Adieu.

I spend much time puzzling over this letter. The tone is abrupt, which is uncharacteristic in itself, but to me, the phrase 'a younger Brother of his' is particularly baffling. At first I wonder whether they are referring to Con's own younger brother, but Ferdinand would have been in his fifties at this point, and as a priest, it seems unlikely that he would have had offspring with claim over the scholarship. There's something about the opacity of this letter's phrasing that bothers me, too. I feel sure that I must be missing something here, something that a qualified scholar would spot, but all I take from this letter are more questions. Like so much of the larger story, this text suggests a complex, living reality lurking beyond it, a reality that is ultimately inscrutable to someone of my distance and inexpertise.

On the first day of 1830, Con's wife Mary died. Aged only fifteen and thirteen, their sons were both studying in Dublin at the time, but it is possible that they were home for Christmas when they learned of their mother's death. Less than a year later, on 5 October 1831, Con's name appears in the marriage announcements of the *Kerry Evening Post* alongside that of his second (or possibly third) wife. 'At Gretna Green, Cornelius O'Leary, Esq., barrister-at-law, to Hannah, daughter of the late Pierce Purcell of Altamira, co Cork, Esq.' Somehow, I find myself doubting this announcement. For one thing, among seven Purcell siblings, Hannah is the only one whose marriage is not noted in any historical record, apart from this single newspaper announcement. Secondly, as a location for their marriage, the Scottish town of Gretna Green – with its reputation as a haven for lovers seeking a hasty marriage – seems distant to the point of suspicion from the area in which the couple both lived. I long for the Bible again, if only to see how Con might have described this marriage himself, but in its absence, I attempt to imagine him, eldest son of Eibhlín Dubh and Art, now in his early sixties, stepping into the cold Scottish sunlight with a new bride on his arm.

—

A whole decade passes without any discernible ripple of this son's life in the texts I can access – no court-cases in the newspapers, no baptismal records for new children. For Con, life grows quiet. He must have been proud of his sons, Goodwin and Cornelius, the younger studying medicine, while Cornelius, like his father, turned towards law. On the front page of the *Connaught Telegraph* on 20 January 1836 this son is described as a barrister and a Catholic. He and Con take to attending political rallies together. In an article of *The Nation* published on 3 June 1843 is an account of a meeting Con attended at The Corn Exchange. Among matters discussed was the proposal of a number of new members of the Repeal movement. When the time comes for Con himself to be proposed to the crowd, Daniel O'Connell proclaims: 'Another lawyer (cheers)! I have the honour to move that Counsellor Cornelius O'Leary be admitted a member. There is no objection to him at all, except that he is a near and dear relative of mine.' The resolution was carried.

In June of 1846, at their home in Dromore, Con's companion and eldest son Cornelius died at the age of thirty-one. Con ordered his father's grave opened, and followed his son's coffin through birdsong and bees over the narrow bridge to Kilcrea Abbey. See Con now, standing on the same soil where his mother once stood, watching his son slowly enter Art's dark room. Overhead, old crows screech and wheel. I see Con turn away from the grave to leave Kilcrea, his hand heavy on the silver stone of the door jamb. Within a couple of months, the grave would be opened again. This time, Con himself would follow his son through that dark door. He was 77 when he died, just five days shy of his birthday. Now three generations of the family lay together, their bones mingling in the final embrace of father and son and father and son. No female name appears on the gravestone, but the absence of a female name is not evidence of the absence of a female presence. Could Eibhlín Dubh be here too?

Having followed her son from the moment of his birth to the moment of his burial, I am saddened that my search has yielded no further clue to her own life – but what had I expected? An act of desperation, such an approach was always doomed to fail. Now, Ferdinand and Eibhlín have both disappeared, Art is dead, Máire Ní Dhuibh is dead, and Con and his eldest son both lie in the dirt of Kilcrea. Although they were all long gone before I ever began to spy on them, I still mourn the point at which I must witness them fall into oblivion once more. The only descendant left to follow now is Eibhlín's grandson, Con's second son. Goodwin Richard Purcell O'Leary, so I look towards him in the hope that he may reveal something of his grandmother that his father could not. I watch him closely to see what he will make of his life, for he is the last of Eibhlín Dubh's line.

Ambitious and precocious, Goodwin was fascinated from a young age by the workings of the human body. Among the many medical graduates from Edinburgh in 1841, he was awarded a gold medal for his achievements. A polyglot, he began to travel through Europe, continuing his studies as he went. Having lost his mother as a child, Goodwin also buried both his elder brother and his father in the space of a single summer. Three years later, in early spring, he married Helena Sugrue, the daughter of a prosperous family of merchants. The couple, both in their late twenties, made their home in Cork city, where he was appointed Professor of Materia Medica at Queen's College, Cork, in the same department of the same university where I would later stand over a cadaver.

In an issue of *The Freeman's Journal* dated 29 July 1858, directly above news of a ten-foot statue of Empress Josephine in transit towards Martinique, I find a list of the 'Latest Arrivals at Finn's Royal Victoria Lake Hotel'. In the picturesque resort of Killarney, new guests included 'Mr and Mrs Purcell

O'Leary'. Helena's hand is tucked in the hinge of her husband's elbow as they stroll through the breakfast room, nodding at their fellow guests: the elegant Miss Le Hunt, Captain Jacob, the Misses Cliffe, George Martin of Boston, and Alderman Bradley of New York. On each table they pass, I set a freshly pressed cloth, silver cutlery, and steam yawning from the china mouth of every teacup.

Back in the city, the couple made their home at 9 Sidney Place. I have stood outside this building, my hand a shade to the sun against which Goodwin and Helena's home rises in three stories of bright red brick. A flight of steps leads from the street to the door and fourteen windows face the city valley below. Beyond each of those windows is a room through which they once moved. Leaving the house on a bright morning with a slender case in one hand and an umbrella hooked over the other, Goodwin's commute to the college would have made for a gentle stroll across the city. As Professor of Materia Medica, he spent his days teaching the therapeutic properties of various substances, and the ways in which they might be used to influence the workings of the human body. The examinations Goodwin set for his students let us glimpse some of the words he might have spoken during his working day.

Explain the re-actions which take place in the prepara-tion of valerianic acid, and trisnitrate of bismuth.

Describe the properties, chemical characteristics, and action of foxglove? Give its Latin name, its preparations, indications, contra-indications, and doses.

What is the physiological action and the uses of cod-liver oil?

—

In western Canada, jagged peaks of limestone and sandstone form a mountainscape that lies deep under pale sheets of snow. Goodwin was among the selec-tion committee that chose Dr James Hector as chief geologist for the expedition team that first mapped this area and, in 1859, Hector named these moun-tains after Eibhlín Dubh's grandson. I can't help but judge the arrogance of a generation of white explorers that presumed to 'name' a mountain range formed in Proterozoic Era, overwriting the nomenclature chosen by the people who had known those slopes for generations, and yet Goodwin's name remains in every modern atlas I find. To place my fingertip on that spot and hold it there on the letters of his name is not only to sense some remnant of his life

– and indeed, of Eibhlín Dubh's – it is also to sense the lives of others. On those slopes, many hearts are beating now: the hearts of grizzly bears snoring in caves and elk strolling under velvet antlers, the hearts of mountain goats and caribou nibbling lichen, the hearts of wolverines and the hearts of meadowlarks swooping over that steep white. Under my finger are the letters of Goodwin's name, and under his name, a pulse still beats.

In 1862, a fire was sparked in the university, a fire that began in the rooms dedicated to Materia Medica. Conspiracies swirled around possible culprits, but for my purposes I am less interested in such accusations, and more in any glimpse that this event might provide to Goodwin's life. In his deposition, Denis Bullen, professor of surgery, described the scene on the day the fire broke out:

> The room was in order, except that I observed, on an open shelf over the door at least one dozen large glass jars were placed, containing Pathological specimens preserved in spirits of wine (some of them methylated spirit).

After the fire had finally been extinguished, Bullen returned, noting,

> On closely inspecting these portions of the floor, I, deponent, saw visible marks, as if an inflammable fluid

(as methylated spirit) had leaked out from under the said door, making a defined figure on the timber flooring, and as if, when this part of the floor took fire, the part impregnated with the fluid burned through.

He also suggested who might be responsible:

> some person intimately acquainted with the tenor of said College, who had accurate knowledge of the peculiar matter contained in the Materia Medica Museum; that he had access thereto, without apprehension of being detected, and went into the said room by ordinary means, thereby evading discovery … It was only necessary to place the manuscripts on the floor, pour over them the contents of a few of the jars, apply an ignited lucifer match, then lock the door.

When I imagine how the hot breath of that fire must have blazed through the medical department, it strikes me as strange that so many years later, its modern quarters might be abbreviated from the Facility for Learning Anatomy Morphology and Embryology to FLAME. Perhaps the past is always trembling inside the present, whether or not we sense it.

The losses sustained in the fire are detailed in *The Cork Constitution* of 16 May 1862:

> One whole wing of the building has been completely gutted, and a valuable pathological museum, which took the diligent labour of years to accumulate, and a

large number of valuables have been utterly destroyed
... Professor O'Leary, in whose room it is said the fire
commenced, is one of the heaviest sufferers, there
having been destroyed eleven years' manuscripts,
besides a valuable microscope, a collection of micro-
scopic preparations made by himself, which were
highly prized, and a number of other articles.

This was the destruction of a life's work, and the more
I learn of his character, the more I feel that the grief
of this loss haunted Eibhlín Dubh's grandson for the
rest of his days.

Goodwin began to struggle. Perhaps he had been
struggling already, but from 1862 onwards, the university archives reveal difficulties with his professional
duties. In 1865 his roll book was not returned, and
then found to be faulty, with absent students marked
in attendance. In seeking to move one of his lecturing
days to Saturday, he cites feeling overworked. Under
the headline 'A SERIOUS BUSINESS', *The Waterford News* reported that Goodwin had involved himself in a scuffle outside a money-lender's office. His
companion, Edward Freeman, was owed money by
William Lindsay, a printer and stationer from Fermoy,
and when

Mr Freeman collared Lindsay and told him that he
had a revolver in his pocket, with which he would

shoot him, Professor O'Leary seized Mr Lindsay by the throat, dashed him against the wall, and waving a horsewhip over his head, threatened to 'flake' him with it if he did not sign the bond.

What might Goodwin's employers have made of this turn of events? What of Helena? How would she have felt to see this behaviour published in the newspaper for all to see – was it a shock to her, a source of shame or indignation, or was this the public culmination of behaviours familiar to the woman who shared a home with him? In 1867 he received correspondence from the president of his workplace querying why his lectures had ended as early in the term as 14 April. Goodwin was not in the room; he had left.

In a newspaper dated 12 May 1869, I find the following account:

Professor Purcell O'Leary, of Queen's College, was spending yesterday evening at an hotel in the city, and his man-servant called for him about eleven o'clock. When passing through Prince's street, three men met them. It is not known what the three men said or did, but the professor pulled out his revolver and presented it at them, whereupon a shout of *police* was raised. The professor then put down the weapon, and approached the three men, to whom he commenced to explain the superior make and shape of the weapon, and its kicking abilities. While this was going on two or three others were attracted to the spot, and while the professor held the revolver in his hand it was seized from behind his back and wrenched out of his hand. A scuffle ensued, in which the professor was struck and knocked down, but he was unable to regain possession of his revolver.

Goodwin's temperament flailed between such strange outbursts and performances of great intellectual clarity. In 1870, the *Cork Examiner* details a guest lecture delivered to the illustrious member of the Literary and Scientific Society:

The lecture was generally admitted to be one of the most brilliant and interesting ever delivered in the theatre of the Institution; technical details which were most lucidly stated, being enlivened by occasional flashes of wit, and humour, by graceful flights of fancy, and passages of quaint eloquence, which evoked loud and frequent applause.

In 1873, the *Cork Constitution* recounts a musical recital in the city, featuring 'Song, "The Colleen Dhu" – Words by Dr. Purcell O'Leary'. 'Dhu' is an abbreviation of 'Dubh'. That same year, *The Bradford Observer* published the headline 'EXTRAORDINARY AFFAIR AT QUEENSTOWN':

Professor Purcell O'Leary, who went like a maniac through the streets of Queenstown on Monday, dressed to represent the Shah of Persia, in a yellow suit and chamois knee breeches, armed with a sword, bow, arrow, and a large club, and wearing a gold crown for a cap, was arrested late in the evening and brought before Messrs Macleod, RM, and Beamish, JP, charged with presenting a revolver at one of his servants, and firing the same at her head. The unfortunate gentleman was walking through the town all day, followed by crowds especially a number of emigrants, who thought he was some sort of wild Indian, and in several instances, made them fly in all directions with his club and arrows. Colonel Lloyd was attacked by him near the Royal Cork Yacht Club, his hat knocked off, and he was obliged to fly for refuge to the Cork Clubhouse. He then went home by train, and encountered a young woman selling strawberries at his house. He met her with a loaded pistol, fired over her head, and nearly frightened the poor creature out of her wits; after which he reduced some of his house furniture to splinters with a sword. He was lodged in Bridewell, on remand, for eight days.

Where had the furniture described as 'his' come from? Might it have been inherited? Heirloom: the impulsive twitch, the rages, the grudges, and the brashness – such traits are not unfamiliar within the broader emotional architecture of this family. With every newspaper report I find, I feel for Helena. Reading the *Sligo Champion* of 5 July 1873, I wince:

> Dr Purcell O'Leary, Professor, Queen's College, Cork, was on Monday evening arrested in Queenstown on a warrant. Informations were made by Mrs O'Leary and her servant Ellen Daly, charging him with repeated acts of violence. He drew a revolver on the servant, and caught his wife by the throat. His violence was so great they were obliged to fly from the house.

By 1875 he had resigned his professorship and gone to England to stay with his mother's brother, the uncle with whom he shared a name. The Reverend Goodwin Purcell had dedicated his life to his congregation in the village of Charlesworth, Derbyshire. There, he raised money to build a modest chapel, a school, and a vicarage. It was in this village with its steep hills and cluster of gritstone buildings that Goodwin Purcell O'Leary, grandson of Eibhlín Dubh, died on a summer Sunday morning, at 9:30 on 9 July 1876. He was fifty-nine years old. His obituary in *The Lancet* allows us a glimpse into his time in England.

> Suffering for the past two years from phthisis, he had retired to Charlesworth in the hope of recruiting his health; and few beyond his own relatives knew the distinguished reputation he had earned, or the talents concealed under his quiet and unobtrusive manner.

'Phthisis', I find, is an archaic term for tuberculosis. Goodwin's uncle was granted the letters of administration of his estate, but the will was annexed and the professor's effects listed as 'less than £100'. When Helena died in 1889, however, she left a fortune of £3,769 9 *s.* 4½ *d.*

The Nation published an account of Goodwin's funeral leaving Manchester

> in a suite of three coffins ... At 7.30 the funeral arrived at Kilcrea Abbey. The procession passed down the beautiful avenue beneath the shadow of the tall elm trees that line it on both sides, Mr. Aldworth reading the service of the Church of England, the group of mourners standing by beneath the tower of the grey ruin, as the evening sun was lighting up the nave, cloisters, and chancel of this historic spot. At the conclusion of the service, the body was lowered into the tomb amidst ancestral ashes, and the vault was then sealed up for time.

The End. Another of his obituaries begins: 'A notable man has passed away from us, whose name and brilliant acquirements deserve more than a passing notice,' and ends with the following line: 'Dr O'Leary's grandfather was married to Miss O'Connell, sister to the grandfather of the late Daniel O'Connell, M.P. of Derrinane Abbey, Co. Kerry.' There she is, at last, our Eibhlín Dubh, marked again as mother and sister.

I have searched and searched through Goodwin's life, hungering for of any trace of her, and then, at the very last moment, *Ta-dah!*, she appears, cast once more in the periphery of men's lives.

Another ending has come upon me, and again, I meet it with reluctance. I have grown fond of this professor, for through him I have witnessed how temperament may ripple through generations. In studying Goodwin's life, I have felt something of Art's ferocity and impulsivity, but I have also felt something of Eibhlín Dubh: her pride, her rage, and her intelligence, as these traits ricocheted through another life.

—

To spend such long periods facing the texts of the past can be dizzying, and it is not always a voyage of reason; the longer one pursues the past, the more unusual the coincidences one observes. As an amateur paddling in a vast ocean of historical research, I doubt myself with each piece of information I find. Any scholarship I find of Eibhlín Dubh's second son suggests that Fear, or Ferdinand, became a priest and disappeared, but I don't believe that this is true, because I find him, I do, and not by skill, but by accident.

The first time he surprises me, I am scanning a ledger of old Marriage Bonds in search of confirmation of his parents' union. Instead, when I reach L for *Leary*, their son leaps out at me. *Ferdinand!* I think, *What are you doing here?* I run my finger over his name and find that I am laughing quietly to myself. Surely it can't be him, I think, surely someone else would have found such a record long before me, and yet, new hope begins to throb in me, red and muscular as a heart. If this is Eibhlín Dubh's son, he might hold a different kind of clue to her life. I run my finger through the other pairs of male and female names, and every time I come to Ferdinand's entry, goose-bumps swim the line of my spine.

Leake, George, and Ann Purcell 1763
Leake, Samuel and Joane Stephens 1680
Leary, Ferdinand, and   *1797*
Leary, Timothy, and Jane Kilpatrick 1720
Lease, Thomas, and Mary Mara 1779
Leaves, Ann, and Robert Law 1796
Lebat, Margaret, and John Reeves 1777

Never in this quest have I found a simple answer; every lead is always a prelude to more questions. Even this document holds a mystery within it – Ferdinand's line is the only one with a lacuna where the woman's name should be. Everywhere I turn, another erasure greets me.

I take the fact that Eibhlín Dubh refers to him as a baby in the *Caoineadh*, and calculate backwards to estimate his year of birth as approximately 1772. This leads me to conclude that this marriage bond would have been drawn up when he was (perhaps) in his mid-twenties. If a marriage followed, however, I cannot find evidence of it. I do, however, stumble upon evidence of another relationship.

This discovery happens while I am intent on finding his older brother, scowling in concentration through church records in search of a baptism record for Con. I do find a Cornelius Leary, but his dates don't match the incarnation I seek: another dead end. I am about to start again when I notice that this baby's father was called Ferdinand. The coincidence of finding these two names in such proximity draws me closer. I follow this father's name through the records, scanning page after digitised page, all the while whispering, 'Ferdinand O'Leary, Ferdinand O'Leary,' repeating it like a summons, or like a spell, to no avail. There is nothing there. Still, I enter the keys: *Search. Return. Search. Return.* Eventually, I return to the original record and note the name of this Cornelius's mother: Cathe, or Catherine Mullane, and set to following her instead, tiptoeing after her as she enters the church again and again, each time with a new baby in her arms. She stands at the baptismal font in 1818, 1820, 1823, 1825, 1828, 1830, 1831, and 1836, and with each new baptism, her partner's name appears differently in the digital transcriptions: now Osmond, now Terdmand, now Frederick. My suspicions are electric enough to send me cross-referencing each of these documents to judge them against the difficult copperplate of the old church ledgers. I run the pale scalpel-scar of my fingertip along those handwritten names, and there, with each new baptism, the father's name is the same.

I am painfully aware, despite my excitement, that I am no scholar, that my presumptions could all be a leap too far, this may not be Eibhlín Dubh's son at all. My evidence is only the evidence of my body – I weep when I see that his first daughter was named Ellen, and two of his sons Arthur and Cornelius. This discovery brings to mind again the vexed letters between his uncles, discussing the educational *bourse* to Paris: 'yet Maurice, Connor tells me that you and your Brothers have nominated a younger Brother of his to the first vacancy'.

Ferdinand married Catherine O'Mullane in St Mary's of Cork city on 9 July 1817. The more I read his wife's name, the more it perplexes me, because in it, I sense an echo whose origin I can't quite pinpoint. It takes weeks before I realise why it sounds so familiar. I once read of another alliance by marriage between the O'Connells of Derrynane and the O'Mullanes of Whitechurch, when Eibhlín Dubh's brother Morgan married a daughter of their family. That their children included the politician Daniel O'Connell means that many academics have already studied this family line, making it easy for me to find his mother, Catherine. She died in her mid-sixties, having survived her husband by nearly a decade. Rather than join him in the O'Connell family plot, she chose to be buried at her own ancestral graveyard at Newberry, under a slab on which her name was engraved as Catherina. I wonder whether Eibhlín Dubh might have chosen a burial among her kin on Abbey Island, and find myself longing again for the Bible in which her son wrote his family history.

It takes over a year, but eventually I find the Bible, or the Bible finds me. I am sitting on the top floor of the city library when it happens, among books so old that they must be locked in glass cabinets, with two men who observe as visitors read. I have returned to double-check a date mentioned by the historian John T. Collins, when I notice that he subsequently published a supplement to his original article on Art's death. How had I missed this? It is in this supplement that I find the Bible, at last, transcribed from Con's hand into type. I read every word, chasing the moment when he will mention his mother, when all my questions will be answered, and I can find peace. My eye gallops the text from beginning to end, and then my head falls to the table with a thunk. In front of two men who watch silently, I start to cry.

I, Cornelius O'Leary was married to Mary Purcell at St Anne's Shandon on 25th day of April 1814 by the Rev. Richard Lee, Curate of said Church. Cornelius Ferdinand Purcell O'Leary was born on 6th day of October 1815 and christened by the Rev. Richard Lee on 11th day of February 1816 by my directions. He was privately baptized on the day of his birth at Glade Cottage, Glanmire, the property of Miss Lily, where we resided from 3rd of October 1815 to 25th of March 1816, having previously resided at No.2 (Grand) Parade Cork. He was confirmed at Newmarket Church by the Right Rev. Dr. Warburton, Bishop of Cloyne on 19th of September 1824. (Died at Upper Dromore on 21st of June, 1846)

Goodwin Richard Purcell O'Leary was born at Clashmorgan Cottage on 19th March 1817. I baptised him an hour after his birth. He was christened by the Rev. Arthur Herbert, Rector of Mourne Abbey at Clashmorgan on 12th July 1817, there being present his aunt, Mrs James Purcell, and his two cousins, Susan and Anne Purcell. It was a private baptism. July 25th 1817. C. O'Leary.

I was born at Rathleigh in the parish of Tohna-droman in the barony of West Muskerry on 28th day of August 1768 (as I have been told), and my father, Arthur O'Leary of said Rathleigh, esq., was shot at Carriganimy on the 4th day of May, 1773. My wife, Mary O'Leary, otherwise Purcell, was born at Springrove on the 18th of March, 1774. Written at Paris. October 1827, Cornelius O'Leary. (In. another hand) She died at Sunday's Well, Cork, on the 1st day of January, 1830.

(The said Cornelius O'Leary, Senr., died at Upper Dromore, aged 77 years, 11 months and 23 days, on the 26th day of August, 1846.)

I make myself read the third paragraph again and again, as though rereading it might somehow squeeze her name from his words. There she is, our Eibhlín, as she is always is: gone. Another erasure from another male text. If I can't find her here, in her own son's hand, then I will find her nowhere. The reasonable part of my brain insists that I give up now, but I still can't stop. What will it take to make me let go?

So many archives have been digitised and opened to online public access by the time I embark on this adventure that my curiosity is not restricted to any opening hours. At 4 AM on a Tuesday I am the only one awake, curled in a blanket, following Art's brother as he runs through our city again and clambers into a boat. I shadow him all the way to America, where his name appears in Farley Grubb's compilation of the many runaway servants, convicts, and apprentices advertised in old issues of the *Pennsylvania Gazette*. Then I follow him up to the door of the chapel he will marry in, watching his name appear in the marriage ledger, letter by letter. I follow him onwards through the lean years until his death so far from home. How many letters might have made their way over an ocean from the rooms of Raleigh to his own hand? How many texts might have flown from the thoughts of those he knew, to land in his own? In a quiet moment, as he turned towards the window, did he ever feel a shadow grow over his skin, and wonder whether he was being hunted or haunted? There would never have been anyone there when he looked up, no brother-ghost, no magistrate, no mercenary seeking a reward; if he felt eyes on him, it was only me, only me. I have followed him as I have followed them all. I followed Eibhlín Dubh until she faded into the gloom. I followed her son Con through three marriages and two sons, then followed each of those sons from birth to the ground. I followed Ferdinand and Cath to the baptismal font again and again, each time pausing to watch a small river ripple through their babies' hair. I have given months of my life to the effort of creeping after these strangers, *and for what?* I remember when I thought that this task would put me in service, somehow, to a woman I admired, but my small skills, self-taught and slapdash, have faltered. I have gone as far as I can.

Perhaps, I think, letting go would be the first true kindness I have shown Eibhlín Dubh. Even in this, I fail. I tell myself again and again that I must release her, but when I lie down to sleep, I grip her nothing-hand so hard that I wake to find four red moons imprinted in my palm.

16. wild bees and their fizzy curiosities

Cion an chroí seo agamsa

All my heart's fondness

—Eibhlín Dubh Ní Chonaill

I. BAD TABBY CAT

An old woman dies, and I arrive at her house with a car full of children and her keys in my handbag. Her home is now ours – as are all the zeroes on our mortgage documents – but the rooms still feel like hers. After the FOR SALE sign has been removed, I hold tight to any small traces I find of this stranger's life – her plastic pegs shivering on the clothes-line, her teacups tucked into each other, neat as dreams, the basket of soft dusting cloths under her sink. Beyond her hangers, the wallpaper she pressed onto the interior of her closets gives them the air of distinct rooms within rooms. I attend tenderly to each of her machines, scrubbing them and setting them whirling once more, resurrecting the clockwork of tumble dryer, microwave, washing machine, and dishwasher, until they are all spinning again. Slat by slat, our flat-packed bed is assembled where hers stood for fifty years; I hope that I will soon hold a new baby here. Twisting the Allen key clockwise to tighten the head-board, I wonder whether I will inherit her dreams.

In the garden is a stray kitten, scrawny and wild. Sweet little thing, I think, lifting her by claw and hiss from her wilderness of brambles. I press her to my chest. The harder she struggles, the harder I squeeze. *Mine*, I think. She spits. I've read that it is a kindness to neuter strays, but when I set to googling local vets I am taken aback by the fee. I arrange an appointment nevertheless, and purchase a sack of cat food and a plastic carry-cage. If this cat costs me money, she also costs me my husband's ire. It's not that he loathes cats, he says, or not *only* that, it's the fact that I continue to foist further responsibilities on us without ever pausing to ask: more babies, more plans, and more pets. I shrug. Let him be angry, she is worth the price. My fierce green-eye, I delight in her delight. When I spy on her tossing the gruesome corpse of a mouse in her paws, puppeting it back to life, I think how alike we are, how alike. She grows fond of me too, and takes to sleeping in our bed, kissing her cheek against my chin every evening until I am drunk on the golden whiskey of my own benevolence. My husband kicks in his sleep.

The calendar carries us to the day when the vet will perform the cat's operation. I lock her in the plastic cage and pay him to knife her and steal all her future kittens. She was right to be suspicious.

When she wakes, she staggers away from me fast, lurching groggily through the garden. I chase her with my arms wide open. *Here, kitty, here kitty-kitty.*

II. WHIRL AND BURBLE

I love the garden and the garden loves me, but it isn't mine, not really. I will always share it with the woman who began it, who arrived in a sun-dress to a newly built council house and cared for this garden all her life. I don't know where she is now, but her bulbs are buried here. The very first morning that I walked through her garden, her daffodils' buttery hellos were easily translated: they nodded. I nodded back.

To work this soil is to sift an archaeology of a stranger's thought. Each time I find an old bulb or the splinters of a broken cup planted for drainage, I am thankful for her labour. With every month, more of her flowers lift their heads from the soil, waving polite hellos in pinks and yellows and blues. I don't know their names, but I think of her in every small act of weeding and pruning, of watering and fertilising. I pat the earth with gentleness. My nails are always dirty, my palms shovel-blistered, my knees drenched, but I don't care. I am happy here. In mapping my own additions to this small plot, I choose with care, because I hold a specific desire for this place: I want to lure the bees to me.

Plastic seed-trays soon proliferate all along our windowsills, each square of soil brimming with a velvet darkness from which tiny seedlings peek. I love the sprouting of their infant limbs, how they wear their seedcases like jaunty bonnets. Outside, my husband thuds a slow metronome, heaving his pickaxe back and crash and back and crash, hacking me a margin of new earth. When we stop for coffee he is quieter than usual, but if I don't pay him much heed, it is only because I am busy thinking of the bees.

Of the many species of bumblebee in Ireland, I've read that one third may be extinct within a decade. The cat watches from the wall as I set to work, a clumsy gardener who digs not by trowel or spade but by dented soup spoon. Every day, I am digging and grunting and raking, heaving compost from the shed, setting plump armfuls of plants and bulbs, and patting them down. Each new plant I choose is both nectar and pollen-heavy, every clump of colour designed to bloom as a lure. Here will be sunflowers and snowdrops, I tell my husband, holding his hand tight, and over there, lavender and fuchsia. Our peripheries will hold hedges of hawthorn and hazel, I'll lure honeysuckle along the walls, and we'll abandon a fat ribbon of untouched wilderness beyond, in which brambles and dandelions will flourish. It will be so beautiful, I say, and press my smiling lips to his in excitement. I am determined to rewrite the air here until it sings the songs of long ago; I want it rewound and purring with bees.

We may imagine that we can imagine the past, but this is an impossibility. As a child I was so enchanted by history that I would sometimes sit by a stream and try to daydream myself back in time. To the hurry-burble of water, my mind set to work, forgiving first the distant buzz of traffic, and then, through clumsy acts of further deletion, trying to subtract all the other resonances of modernity. This, I told my ears, this soundscape, yes, but minus cars, minus tractors, minus airplanes, minus the sad cow-howl of industrial farming, minus it all, until only stream-lilt and bird-chirp remain. Now, I would tell myself, this, *this* must have been what the past really sounded like. I was wrong. Long ago, the air was never as quiet as I presumed. It was alive, strumming the tune of those sisters so accustomed to drudgery, the background chorus of those who always hum as they work.

III. AN OPENING OPENING

As the new plants unfurled into sunlight, the bees began to arrive. I dragged a cobwebbed lawn-chair from the garage and spied on their busy rumps as they browsed the gifts I'd grown for them. The cat padded over to sniff my shin. I watched the bees and thought of the poet Paula Meehan. I'd heard her describe how cherished bees were in medieval Ireland, when entire tracts of our Brehon laws provided a legal framework for their behaviour. On a cockled vellum page of the fourteenth-century volume *Senchus Mór* in Trinity College, some of those old Bechbretha directives survived. Should a person happen upon a roving cloud of bees, it said, they could legally adopt it. Should a swarm be found trespassing, they would be allowed some seasons to mooch about freely, but if such pollen thievery continued into a fourth year, the neighbour would be due a swarm of her own as compensation. Bees flew through the law and into folklore. I overheard their song in one of my favourite stories from the *Schools' Collection* archives, transcribed in Waterford in the 1930s. Siobhán Ní Lonáin was thirteen when she copied this tale from her mother's voice to paper, a female text in flight. I translate it as follows:

> Long ago, deep inside the cliffs at An Rinn, there was a lios. One day a man clambered down, not knowing what was within. Suddenly, the cliff opened and hundreds of bees flew out. Then a small man emerged and brought him inside the cliff and down a tall stairs. At the bottom was a room where he found many fairies, all singing and dancing. For three years, he was held there, and when at last he left, they gave him a pot of gold. I got this story from my mother. Age 40.

Whenever I return to this tale I feel it surge into a vessel of sound. Rewind it. Listen again, now: hear the heave and hurt of the sea, the cold drip of the cliff smeared with pale splatters, a man's breath, torn and tearing as he clambers down the stone, all grunt and grip and grunt and grip, and beyond those sounds of human exertion, beyond the rage-squawks of seabirds, beyond the little give and sing of pebbles, another sound is beginning. It comes from within – no – it *hums* from within, from the unfathomable distance that exists in the cliff's depths, through all its hidden caves and chambers. The man senses the sound before he hears it. He feels the air glitch in his fingertips, a sudden rumbling in his chest, and a resonance behind his breastbone. Still, he clings to the stone. Now the cliff is rasping itself ajar with a heave, and he watches, agog, as that crack grows, an opening, opening. Within, rushing fast, faster than drizzle, a city of bees is in motion. The lush hum of a single bee is a sound we can conjure easily, but we must magnify that sound now, through repeated multiplication. More. More. Listen: here they come.

The man enters.

The cliff closes.

All the years he is locked inside that architecture of hive and honeycomb go unspoken. The seasons spin on without him. When finally he succeeds in escaping those rooms of dance and song and enchanted bees, his parting gift is – what else? – gold. He tucks that sweet glow under his oxter as he strides out of the cliff and out of this story, into some future plot we listeners are not privy to. The final words of this text occur in an utterance that is at once simple, and yet holds such power: 'I got this story from my mother.'

IV. WHAT I COULDN'T BEAR TO TELL THE BEES

There is so much more to this old tale that I long to know. What was the man doing out on a cliff in the first place? Where did the bees go? Do his kin still tell this story of his, or has it been forgotten? Do the ancestors of those bees still wander that same cliff, fumbling through honeysuckle bells?

The marginal plot of the bees is so much more interesting to me than the man's triumphant acquisition of gold, and yet they are so quickly abandoned as peripheral characters in favour of the human narrative. The first question I would ask Siobhán's mother would be, 'What happened to the bees?' I can imagine her exasperated answer, as she hurries on to her next task. 'They're only bees.'

They are only bees, it's true. In the absence of the neurological embellishments that make moral beings of humans, we assume other creatures' lives – their unique imperatives and plots – are somehow lesser by comparison with our own. However, a bee, being a bee, will accept her own death to let her sister bees live, a decision with which any human would surely struggle. The opposite of selfishness, this – if she stings, it is to protect others from danger, knowing that she will soon fall, sputtering in the dirt, donating her life so that others may survive.

How lonesome I'd be, if the bees left the sweet-shop I've built for them. I've done all I can to hearten them, I have hummed to them, I have fed and sheltered and loved them. I want to keep them here at all costs – even if it means lying to them. 'Tell the bees,' people used to say, 'tell them of any bereavement, any family change, you must tell the bees or they'll fly away.' I had a secret I knew I should tell the bees, but I'd kept it to myself, because I would stop at nothing to prevent them from leaving.

What I couldn't bear to tell them was that my husband was intent on ending the growth of our family. He wanted a vasectomy. If he had his way, all the future babies I had been wishing for would be deleted. His reasons were many and complex. Mine, on the other hand, sounded so superficial that I cringed hearing myself say them aloud, and yet, I asked the same question over and over again, always with my head tilted sadly. 'But what about me? I want another baby,' I would say, addressing my greedy question to his pale face and his drained, dark-ringed gaze. He always shook his head. I sulked in bed with the cat purring on my chest, trying to dream up some way to deter him.

This was a man who fainted giving a blood sample; the mere mention of a needle made him clench his fists. I'd seen him shudder whenever such procedures were mentioned on TV. I'd seen him cross his legs; I'd seen his wince. I tried to use these fears to weaken his resolve, asking again and again if he had considered the gory reality of the procedure, but he knew me too well, he saw through my scheming, and simply shrugged. 'You're being so selfish,' I said. 'Am I?' he replied. 'Think about it.'

I did. I could see how he had married a woman who loved the drug of birth, who habitually drowned herself in nursling-love, a woman who flung herself to her knees in housework, and merrily made of herself a shadow to the tyranny of lists. When he looked at our family he saw an exhausted mother already stretched too thin, and a cluster of children who needed more of their parents, not less of less of less. *Think about it,* he'd said, and the more I did, the more I understood his argument. It may be unpleasant when another claims to understand one's needs better than oneself, but it is excruciating to realise that they are correct in their assessment, and that they wish to help, even if doing so means inflicting surgery on themselves. His eyes were love-lit when he explained that in choosing this procedure, he might free us both from exhaustion, that for the first time in a decade, we would have no milk-broken sleep, no more bouts of fever-teeth, and no more nappies. I wanted to ask what I would do without a baby to attend to, but I couldn't bring myself to interrupt him. He had watched me birth four children by scalpel, and now he was calling for the blade to be brought to his own body. *Once and for all*, he had said. *For all*. I was beginning to see what he meant – if his decision was selfish, it was selfless as well.

V. SNIP-SNIP/LIMP-LIMP

Making our way to the clinic, my sighs grow frequent. My husband parks and kisses me as our daughter snores in her car seat. I meet his eye. 'Are you sure?' I ask. 'Yes. Yes! You wait here. I'll be back soon.' He smiles and, with that, he leaves.

I sulk, ripping open the purple foil of a Twirl and slamming the chocolate on its inner silver, chewing crossly while swiping my phone. I gorge myself on bullet-points of vasectomy until I can create a vision of what might be occurring in that room. I imagine a doctor with a therapeutic grin, a white coat, and a jaunty moustache, which I twirl at either end. I set him applying anaesthetic to my husband's scrotum, then I put a silver scissors in one of his hands and a needle in the other. He snips through skin while my husband averts his eyes, dodging the sight of an opening opening. With a deft and practised pinch, then, he finds a minuscule tube under the skin and tugs it cleanly from his balls, unspooling it as firmly as a seamstress tugs thread. Just before the doctor severs the thread that bound us to all our future children, my husband might feel the air glitch a little in his fingertips. *Snip* goes the evil scissors, *snip-snip*, and the doctor nods and fixes it with a tiny surgical clip. There are still stitchings and dressings and debriefings to be dreamt up, but I have been too slow in my imaginings, because *limp* goes my husband, *limp-limp* into the car park towards where I sit, wiping chocolate from my lips, feeling suddenly tender towards this thief of children. Watching his slow, bruised return, he seems almost to hover. If altruism may be interpreted as prioritising others' wellbeing over one's own physical comfort, then I am watching it in motion now, pure and holy, sidestepping an empty crisp packet, grimacing towards me.

In this moment, I am a very reluctant recipient of another's gift. I do not want it, this gesture of his, I want nothing to do with this ending. But despite how strongly I raged against it, I find that I can't quite resent it anymore. This decision, and the physical pain he has endured in proceeding with it, are a strange sort of gift. He is not only freeing himself, he is snipping me free too. If I cannot hold another infant, then maybe I will begin to grow something else – something I can't imagine yet.

VI. TELL

I couldn't keep the secret for long, not from my precious bees. Much as I loved him, I knew that I'd have to report him for what he'd done. I found them stumbling through the purple parlours of foxgloves. There, I rehearsed what I'd say: that my husband had chosen a blade over us, and that our family would never grow, now, as I'd hoped, that I loved him more than ever before, but I was also filled with sorrow. My lips quivered a little in ugly self-pity as I prepared to speak, but then I saw that the bees would hold no sympathy for me. I should have listened more closely to the hum of their daily return. Such are their mysterious judgments – they guessed my message before I spoke, and simply nodded. They stayed.

17. how blurred the furze

dúnta suas go dlúth
mar a bheadh glas a bheadh ar thrúnc
's go raghadh an eochair amú.

keeping it sealed so tightly
as a lock clasps a chest
whose golden key has been lost from me.

—Eibhlín Dubh Ní Chonaill

AS A HEART HOLDS its chambers, as a poem holds its verses, so a house holds its rooms. Within, a throbbing presence comes and goes. In one room is a mirror in which a woman's reflection is scrubbing a sink. She pauses, then bends to peer into her most cherished room of all. Perhaps it is the old wallpaper that gives this cupboard the distinct air of a room within a room, an echo of another she once knew, cast again here in miniature, for beyond its door lies a breast-pump in a crumpled bag. Little engine, little pulse, tenderly dismantled and packed up, it rests here in silence, its cord long disconnected from its source. To look at it is to conjure again its old purr and hiss: a remembered chorus. The right thing to do would be to relinquish it to someone who'd make better use of it, but I can't imagine myself without its presence, any more than I can imagine my life without Eibhlín Dubh.

When I first dedicated my days to searching for hers, I hoped that I might honour her by placing myself in service to her. Only now do I see how much she has given to me in return. Before my life collided with hers, so many of my hours were spent skittering between the twin demands of milk and lists that I hadn't noticed how blurred the furze had grown around me. Now I delight in the yellow petals jigging in the breeze, in every thorn-tip, and even in the bare gaps between them. Some parts of Eibhlín Dubh's life, I know now, will always remain hidden to me, no matter how closely I look. Instead of resenting the many lacunae where I have not been able to find her, my hand has learned to hover over those gaps in awe. My attempt to know another woman has found its ending not in the satisfaction of neat discovery, but in the persistence of mystery.

These years have shown me an oblique kind of holding – I have held her and held her, only to find that she holds me too, close as ink on paper and steady as a pulse. Only now do I see that I can't continue to grip her like this, in quiet selfishness. If I could find a way to communicate all I have learned of her days, maybe others would discover the clues that eluded me, and I might learn more of her from them. To do so, I would have to give something very precious away. I would also have to surrender to an ending.

—

On my final sunlit evening in Kilcrea, my daughter gallops ahead of me, clambering between stones, darting fast until she is out of sight and I am alone again, chasing the sound of her voice.

I stride from nave to chancel and catch her close, piggybacking her to the tomb where Eibhlín's men lie together: husband, son, grandsons; skull, skull, skull, skull. Could she be here too, her finger-bones among theirs, all held in the same disarticulated dark? Perhaps. Perhaps not. I remind myself why I have come. I close my eyes to see. I say her name. I thank Eibhlín Dubh. I say all that needs to be said, feeling each word float away from me on the breeze.

My daughter giggles as she twists from my grip and then she is off again, leaping and squealing. I don't want to leave, not yet, but I worry that such exuberant bellowing may upset some unseen mourner, so I sigh and swing her high and turn us towards our car. She throws back her head, fists thumping my breastbone, her voice loud and hot in my ear, bellowing, 'DON'T GO. STAY. STAY.' Through the gate and along the avenue once bounded by skulls, she continues to shout. I press the key and somewhere beyond the boundary wall, the car unlocks itself to my scarred fingertip. Heaving the door open by knee and by shoulder-bone, I click her into her car seat, my voice cold. 'That's enough of that. We are leaving, so be quiet. Good girl.'

Leaving Kilcrea, I regret my stern words, and my gaze seeks hers in the rear-view mirror. Under our freckles, our cheeks are both ember-bright, but her eyelids have fallen closed. Although her roar still surges through my thoughts, she is already elsewhere.

I don't want to go. I drive slow. When I get home, I think, maybe I'll try to cheer myself up by opening a new notebook from my stash. This time, I won't let myself begin by writing *Hoover* or *Sheets* or *Mop* or *Pump*. Instead, I'll think of new words, and then I'll follow them. As I turn the bend towards home, I find that I already know the echo with which that first page will begin.

This is a female text.

caoineadh airt uí laoghaire

---

the keen for art ó laoghaire

i.

Mo ghrá go daingean tú!
Lá dá bhfaca thú
ag ceann tí an mhargaidh,
thug mo shúil aire duit,
thug mo chroí taitneamh duit,
d'éalaíos óm charaid leat
i bhfad ó bhaile leat.

ii.

Is domhsa nárbh aithreach:
chuiris parlús á ghealadh dhom,
rúmanna á mbreacadh dhom,
bácús á dheargadh dhom,
brící á gceapadh dhom,
rósta ar bhearaibh dhom,
mairt á leagadh dhom;
codladh i gclúmh lachan dhom
go dtíodh an t-eadartha
nó thairis dá dtaitneadh liom.

iii.

Mo chara go daingean tú!
Is cuimhin lem' aigne
an lá breá earraigh úd,

i.

O my belovèd, steadfast and true!
The day I first saw you
by the market's thatched roof,
how my eye took a shine to you,
how my heart took delight in you,
I fled my companions with you,
to soar far from home with you.

ii.

And never did I regret it,
for you set a parlour gleaming for me,
bedchambers brightened for me,
an oven warming for me,
plump loaves rising for me,
meats twisting on spits for me,
beef butchered for me,
and duck-down slumbers for me
until midday-milking, or beyond
if I'd want.

iii.

O my companion, steadfast and true!
My mind summons again
that spring afternoon:

gur bhreá thíodh hata dhuit
faoi bhanda óir tarraingthe;
claíomh cinn airgid,
lámh dheas chalma,
rompsáil bhagarthach –
fír-chritheagla
ar namhaid chealgach –
tú i gcóir chun falaracht
is each caol ceannann fút.
D'umhlaídís Sasanaigh
síos go talamh duit,
is ní ar mhaithe leat
ach le haon-chorp eagla,
cé gur leo a cailleadh tú,
a mhuirnín mh'anama …

iv.
A mharcaigh na mbán-ghlac!
Is maith thíodh biorán duit,
daingean faoi cháimbric,
is hata faoi lása.
Tar éis teacht duit thar sáile,
glantaí an tsráid duit,
is ní le grá dhuit,
ach le han-chuid gráine ort.

how handsome, your hat
with the golden trim,
the silver hilt gripped
in your firm fist,
your swagger so menacing
it set enemies trembling
as their foe approached,
oh, and below, the blaze
of your slender mare glowed.
Even the English would bow before you,
bow down to the ground –
moved not by respect,
but by terrible dread – and yet,
by them you'd soon be struck dead,
o my soul's sweet belovèd.

iv.
O, my bright-handed horseman,
how well it suited you, the pin
pressed in cambric, fixed fast,
and your hat, lace-wrapped.
When you returned from overseas,
the streets cleared for you instantly,
all enemies would flee, and not for fondness,
but in deep animosity.

v.

Mo chara thú go daingean!
Is nuair thiocfaidh chugham abhaile
Conchubhar beag an cheana
is Fear Ó Laoghaire, an leanbh,
fiafróid díom go tapaidh
cár fhágas féin a n-athair.
'Neosad dóibh fé mhairg
gur fhágas i gCill na Martar.
Glaofaidh siad ar a n-athair,
is ní bheidh sé acu le freagairt ...

vi.

Mo chara is mo ghamhain tú!
Gaol Iarla Antroim,
is Bharraigh ón Allchoill,
is breá thíodh lann duit,
hata faoi bhanda,
bróg chaol ghallda,
is culaith den abhras
a sníomhthaí thall duit.

vii.

Mo chara thú go daingean!
Is níor chreideas riamh dod mharbh

v.

O, my steady companion!
When they come home to me,
our dotey little Conchubhar
and Fear Ó Laoghaire, the babba,
I know they'll ask me fast
where I've left their Dada.
Wretchedly, I'll tell them
that I left him in Kilnamartra,
but no matter how they roar
their father will never answer ...

vi.

O, my companion, my bull calf!
Kin of the Earl of Antrim
and the Barrys of Alkill,
how well your sword became you
with that banded hat,
your slender boots of foreign leather,
and the suit of fine couture
stitched and spun abroad for you.

vii.

O, my steady companion!
Never could I have believed you deceased,

gur tháinig chugham do chapall
is a srianta léi go talamh,
is fuil do chroí ar a leacain
siar go t'iallait ghreanta
mar a mbítheá id shuí 's id sheasamh.
Thugas léim go tairsigh,
an dara léim go geata,
an triú léim ar do chapall.

viii.
Do bhuaileas go luath mo bhasa
is do bhaineas as na reathaibh
chomh maith is a bhí sé agam,
go bhfuaras romham tú marbh
cois toirín ísil aitinn,
gan Pápa, gan easpag,
gan cléireach, gan sagart
do léifeadh ort an tsailm,
ach seanbhean chríonna chaite
do leath ort binn dá fallaing –
do chuid fola leat 'na sraithibh;
is níor fhanas le hí ghlanadh
ach í ól suas lem basaibh.

until she came to me, your steed,
with her reins trailing the cobbles,
and your heart's blood smeared from cheek
to saddle, where you'd sit
and even stand, my daredevil.
Three leaps, I took – the first to the threshold,
the second to the gate,
the third to your mare.

viii.
Fast, I clapped my hands,
and fast, fast, I galloped,
fast as ever I could have,
until I found you before me, murdered
by a hunched little furze
with no Pope, no bishop,
no clergy, no holy man
to read your death-psalms,
only a crumpled old hag
who'd draped you in her shawl-rag.
Love, your blood was spilling in cascades,
and I couldn't wipe it away, couldn't clean it up, no,
no, my palms turned cups and oh, I gulped.

ix.

Mo ghrá thú go daingean!
Is éirigh suas id' sheasamh
is tar liom féin abhaile,
go gcuirfeam mairt á leagadh,
go nglaofam ar chóisir fhairsing,
go mbeidh againn ceol á spreagadh,
go gcóireod duitse leaba
faoi bhairlíní geala,
faoi chuilteanna breátha breaca,
a bhainfidh asat allas
in ionad an fhuachta a ghlacais.

x.Deirfiúr Art:
Mo chara is mo stór tú!
Is mó bean chumtha chórach
ó Chorcaigh na seolta
go Droichead na Tóime,
do thabharfadh macha mór bó dhuit
agus dorn buí-óir duit,
ná raghadh a chodladh 'na seomra
oíche do thórraimh.

ix.
O my belovèd, steadfast!
Rise up now, do, stand,
come home with me, hand in hand,
where I'll order cows slaughtered,
and call a banquet so vast,
with music surging loud and fast.
I'll have a bed dressed
in bright blankets
and embellished quilts,
to spark your sweat and set it spilling
until it chases the chill that you've been given.

x. Art's sister:
O, my darling, my pal,
many's the lady – buxom and chic –
from Cork of tall sails
all the way to Toomsbridge
who'd have brought you pastures of cattle
and gold by the fistful,
and not one among them would have dared doze
on the night of your wake, as you lay cold.

xi. Eibhlín Dubh
Mo chara is m'uan tú!
Is ná creid sin uathu,
ná an cogar a fuarais,
ná an scéal fir fuatha,
gur a chodladh a chuas-sa.
Níor throm suan dom:
ach bhí do linbh ró-bhuartha,
's do theastaigh sé uathu
iad a chur chun suaimhnis.

xii.
A dhaoine na n-ae istigh,
'bhfuil aon bhean in Éirinn,
ó luí na gréine,
a shínfeadh a taobh leis,
do bhéarfadh trí lao dhó,
ná raghadh le craobhacha
i ndiaidh Airt Uí Laoghaire
atá anso traochta
ó mhaidin inné agam?

xi. Eibhlín Dubh
O, my friend and my lamb!
Don't you believe that old babble,
the overheard whispers
and hateful scandals
that claim I was napping.
No slumber hampered me, it was only
that your children were so distressed,
and they wept for your presence
to soothe them to rest.

xii.
O noble kin, listen,
is there in all of Ireland any woman,
having spent sunsets
stretched next to him,
having carried three calves for him,
who wouldn't be tormented
after losing Art Ó Laoghaire,
he who lies so cold here now
since early yesterday, when he was ground down?

xiii.

A Mhorrisín léan ort!-
Fuil do chroí is t'ae leat!
Do shúile caochta!
Do ghlúine réabtha!-
A mhairbh mo lao-sa,
is gan aon fhear in Éirinn
a ghreadfadh na piléir leat.

xiv.

Mo chara thú 's mo shearc!
Is éirigh suas, a Airt,
léimse in airde ar t'each,
éirigh go Magh Chromtha isteach,
is go hInse Geimhleach ar ais,
buidéal fíona id ghlaic –
mar a bhíodh i rúm do dhaid.

xv.

M'fhada-chreach léan-ghoirt
ná rabhas-sa taobh leat
nuair lámhadh an piléar leat,
go ngeobhainn é im' thaobh dheas
nó i mbinn mo léine,

xiii.

Morris, you runt; on you, I wish anguish! –
May bad blood spurt from your heart and
    your liver!
Your eyes grow glaucoma!
Your knee-bones both shatter!
You who slaughtered my bull calf,
and not a man in all of Ireland
who'd dare shoot you back.

xiv.

O my friend and my heart!
Rise up now, dear Art,
hop up on your mare, do,
trot in to Macroom,
then on to Inchigeelagh and back
with a wine bottle in hand,
as you always had at home with your Dad.

xv.

An ache, this salt-sorrow of mine,
that I was not by your side
when that bullet came flying,
I'd have seized it here in my right side,
or here, in my blouse's pleats, anything,

is go léigfinn cead slé' leat
a mharcaigh na ré-ghlac.

xvi. Deirfiúr Art:
Mo chreach ghéarchúiseach
ná rabhas ar do chúlaibh
nuair lámhadh an púdar,
go ngeobhainn é im' chom dheas
nó i mbinn mo ghúna,
is go léigfinn cead siúil leat
a mharcaigh na súl nglas,
ós tú b'fhearr léigean chucu.

xvii.
Mo chara thú is mo shearc-mhaoin!
Is gránna an chóir a chur ar ghaiscíoch
comhra agus caipín,
ar mharcach an dea-chroí
a bhíodh ag iascaireacht ar ghlaisíbh
agus ag ól ar hallaíbh
i bhfarradh mná na ngeal-chíoch.
Mo mhíle mearaí
mar a chailleas do thaithí.

anything to let you gallop free,
o bright-grasped horseman, my dear.

xvi. Art's sister:
This raw regret is mine:
that I wasn't there too, just behind
when that gunpowder blew bright.
I'd have seized it here, in my right side,
or here, in my gown's deep pleats,
anything to let you to stride away free,
oh grey-gazed horseman,
learnèd and gentlemanly.

xvii.
O, my friend, my belovèd-treasure!
How grotesque to witness
the grimace of death-cap and coffin
on my kind-hearted horseman,
he who fished the green streams
and drank in grand mansions
with bright-breasted ladies.
Oh, my thousand bewilderments,
I'm dizzied by the loss of your company.

xviii.

Greadadh chughat is díth
a Mhorris ghránna an fhill
a bhain díom fear mo thí,
athair mo leanbh gan aois:
dís acu ag siúl an tí,
's an triú duine acu istigh im chlí,
agus is dócha ná cuirfead díom.

xix.

Mo chara thú is mo thaitneamh!
Nuair ghabhais amach an geata
d'fhillis ar ais go tapaidh,
do phógais do dhís leanbh,
do phógais mise ar bharra baise.
Dúraís, 'A Eibhlín, éirigh id' sheasamh
agus cuir do ghnó chun taisce
go luaimneach is go tapaidh.
Táimse ag fágáil an bhaile,
is ní móide go deo go gcasfainn.'
Níor dheineas dá chaint ach magadh,
mar bhíodh á rá liom go minic cheana.

xviii.

Trouncings and desolations on you,
ghastly Morris of the treachery,
you who thieved my man from me,
the father of my babies,
the pair who walk our home steadily,
and the third, still within me,
I fear will never breathe.

xix.

O, my friend and my pleasure!
Through the gateway, you were leaving
when you turned back swiftly
and kissed your two babies.
Heart of the palm, your kiss for me,
and when you said, 'Rise, Eibhlín,
settle your affairs neatly,
be firm about it, move quickly.
I must leave the home of our family,
and I may never return to ye,'
oh, I only chuckled in mockery,
since you'd made such warnings so frequently.

xx.

Mo chara thú is mo chuid!
A mharcaigh an chlaímh ghil,
éirigh suas anois,
cuir ort do chulaith
éadaigh uasail ghlain,
cuir ort do bhéabhar dubh,
tarraing do lámhainní umat.
Siúd í in airde t'fhuip;
sin í do láir amuigh.
Buail-se an bóthar caol úd soir
mar a maolóidh romhat na toir,
mar a gcaolóidh romhat an sruth,
mar a n-umhlóidh romhat mná is fir,
má tá a mbéasa féin acu –
's is baolach liomsa ná fuil anois …

xxi.

Mo ghrá thú is mo chumann!
's ní hé a bhfuair bás dem chine,
ná bás mo thriúr clainne;
ná Domhnall Mór Ó Conaill,
ná Conall a bháigh an tuile,
ná bean na sé mblian 's fiche
do chuaigh anonn thar uisce
'déanamh cairdeasaí le ríthe –

xx.

O, my friend and my lover!
Dear horseman of the bright sword,
rise up now,
pull on your uniform
of noble, bright cloth
and the dark beaver-skin,
then tug up your gloves.
Look, your whip is hung up above.
Your mare waits beyond.
Hit that narrow road east
where each tree will kneel for you,
each stream will narrow for you,
and all men and women will bow for you,
if they remember the old manners,
though I fear they no longer do ...

xxi.

O, my friend, my companion,
neither my deceased kin,
nor my family's three dead belovèds –
not Domhnall Mór Ó Conaill,
nor Conall drowned by flooding,
not even the twenty-six-year-old lady
who went overseas
to become a companion to royalty –

ní hiad go léir atá agam dá ngairm,
ach Art a bhaint aréir dá bhonnaibh
ar inse Charraig an Ime!
Marcach na lárach doinne
atá agam féin anso go singil –
gan éinne beo 'na ghoire
ach mná beaga dubha an mhuilinn,
is mar bharr ar mo mhíle tubaist
gan a súile féin ag sileadh.

xxii.
Mo chara is mo lao thú!
A Airt Uí Laoghaire
Mhic Conchubhair, Mhic Céadaigh,
Mhic Laoisigh Uí Laoghaire,
aniar ón nGaortha
is anoir ón gCaolchnoc,
mar a bhfásaid caora
is cnó buí ar ghéagaibh
is úlla 'na slaodaibh
'na n-am féinig.
Cárbh ionadh le héinne
dá lasadh Uíbh Laoghaire
agus Béal Átha an Ghaorthaigh
is an Guagán naofa
i ndiaidh mharcaigh na ré-ghlac

oh no one else do I grieve now,
but my own Art, struck down at dusk
and torn from us!
Only the brown mare's horseman
do I still hold, he, alone –
and now none will come close,
only the dark-cloaked little mill-women,
and to multiply my thousand cataclysms,
not one of them will summon a tear for him.

xxii.
O, my friend and my bull calf!
Dear Art Ó Laoghaire,
son of Conor, son of Keady,
son of old Laoiseach Ó Laoghaire
from back west in The Gearagh,
of those who came east from sheer peaks
where sheep grow plump, and branches
grow heavy with clusters of nuts,
where apples spill lush
when their sweet season rises up.
What wonder, now, to anyone
should they all blaze up, all the people
of Iveleary, Ballingeary,
and those of Gougane Barra's holy streams,
howling in grief for our steady-handed horseman,

a mbíodh an fiach á thraochadh
ón nGreanaigh ar saothar
nuair stadaidís caol-choin?
Is a mharcaigh na gclaon-rosc –
nó cad d'imigh aréir ort?
Óir do shíleas féinig
ná maródh an saol tú
nuair cheannaíos duit éide.

xxiii. Deirfiúr Art:
Mo chara thú is mo ghrá!
Gaol mhathshlua an stáit,
go mbíodh ocht mbanaltraí déag ar aon chlár,
go bhfaighidís go léir a bpá –
loilíoch is láir,
cráin 's a hál,
muileann ar áth,
ór buí is airgead bán,
síodaí is bheilbhit bhreá,
píosaí tailimh eastáit,
go nídís cíocha tál
ar lao na mascalach mbán.

he who exhausted the hunt
that day in Grenagh, when his exertions were such
that even the most muscular hounds gave up?
And o, my horseman of firm stare,
what went awry last night?
I never imagined
as I chose your clothes – so elegant and fine –
that you could ever be torn from this life.

xxiii. Art's Sister:
O, my pal, o, my brother!
Kin of nobility,
you kept eighteen wet nurses toiling
and they each earned their salary,
paid in heifers and mares,
in sows and in piglets,
in mills fording rivers,
in bright golds and silvers,
in silks and in velvets,
in vast estate pastures –
all that suckling staff
who worked to serve our fine bull calf.

xxiv.

Mo ghrá is mo rún tú!
'S mo ghrá mo cholúr geal!
Cé ná tánag-sa chughat-sa
is nár thugas mo thrúip liom,
níor chúis náire siúd liom
mar bhíodar i gcúngrach
i seomraí dúnta
is i gcomhraí cúnga,
is i gcodladh gan mhúscailt.

xxv.

Mara mbeadh an bholgach
is an bás dorcha
is an fiabhras spotaitheach,
bheadh an marc-shlua borb san
is a srianta á gcrothadh acu
ag déanamh fothraim
ag teacht dod' shochraid
a Airt an bhrollaigh ghil ...

xxvi.

Mo ghrá thú is mo thaitneamh!
Gaol an mharc-shlua ghairbh
a bhíodh ag lorg an ghleanna,

xxiv.

O my love and my dear!
O my love and my bright dove!
Though I could neither come to your aid
nor bring troops your way,
that's no cause for shame –
for they were all restrained
in their dark place, locked
in coffins and tightly sealed
by wakeless sleep.

xxv.

Were it not for the smallpox,
the Black Death
and the fever-spots,
those gruff hordes would surely have come,
shaking their reins
and raising glorious tumult
as they arrived at your funeral,
dear Art, whose chest was once luminous ...

xxvi.

O, my belovèd, my pleasure!
Kin to the rough horde
who hunted the gorge,

mar a mbainteá astu casadh,
á mbreith isteach don halla,
mar a mbíodh faobhar á chur ar sceanaibh,
muiceoil ar bord á gearradh,
caoireoil ná comhaireofaí a heasnaí,
coirce craorach ramhar
a bhainfeadh sraoth as eachaibh –
capaill ghruagach' sheanga
is buachaillí 'na n-aice
ná bainfí díol ina leaba
ná as fásach a gcapall
dá bhfanaidís siúd seachtain,
a dheartháir láir na gcarad.

xxvii.
Mo chara is mo lao thú!
Is aisling trí néallaibh
do deineadh aréir dom
i gCorcaigh go déanach
ar leaba im' aonar:
gur thit ár gcúirt aolda,
gur chríon an Gaortha,
nár fhan friotal id' chaol-choin
ná binneas ag éanaibh,
nuair fuaradh tú traochta
ar lár an tslé' amuigh,

310

how you led them twisting and turning,
all, then steered them back to the hall,
where blades were sharpening
over pork set for carving,
with countless ribs of mutton,
and oats so tasty
they'd draw speed from each steed,
the stallions, slender and thick-maned,
all attended by stable-boys with care,
and not a soul charged for their beds,
for expenses, or for board of their horses,
even should they stay for a week's rest,
o dear brother of many friends.

xxvii.
O, my friend and my calf!
Last night, such clouded reveries
appeared to me, come midnight
in Cork as I lay awake late.
Alone, I dreamt
our bright-limed home tumbling,
the Gearagh all withering,
without a growl left of your hounds
nor the sweet chirp of birds,
like when I found you
out on that mountain ground,

gan sagart, gan cléireach,
ach seanbhean aosta
do leath binn dá bréid ort
nuair fuadh den chré thú,
a Airt Uí Laoghaire,
is do chuid fola 'na slaodaibh
i mbrollach do léine.

xxviii.
Mo ghrá is mo rún tú!
'S is breá thíodh súd duit,
stoca chúig dhual duit,
buatais go glúin ort,
Caroilín cúinneach,
is fuip go lúfar
ar ghillín shúgach –
is mó ainnir mhodhúil mhúinte
bhíodh ag féachaint sa chúl ort.

xxix.
Mo ghrá go daingean tú!
'S nuair théitheá sna cathracha
daora, daingeana,
bhíodh mná na gceannaithe
ag umhlú go talamh duit,

with neither priest nor clergy
to keep you company, only the crumpled old lady
who folded her cloak over your body.
That soil clung to you fiercely
dear Art Ó Laoghaire,
as your blood drenched streams
through your shirt so bleakly.

xxviii.
O, my love and my darling!
You looked so striking
in your five-folded stockings,
with your boots, knee-high,
and your hat, the cornered Caroline.
Whenever you flicked your whip,
nimble-quick on a merry gelding,
many modest gentlewomen
found their eyes shyly following.

xxix.
O my belovèd, steadfast and true!
When you strolled
those fine city avenues,
merchants' wives always
stooped their curtsies low for you.

óir do thuigidís 'na n-aigne
gur bhreá an leath leaba tú,
nó an bhéalóg chapaill tú,
nó an t-athair leanbh tú.

xxx.

Tá fhios ag Íosa Críost
ná beidh caidhp ar bhathas mo chinn,
ná léine chnis lem thaoibh,
ná bróg ar thrácht mo bhoinn,
ná trioscán ar fuaid mo thí,
ná srian leis an láir ndoinn,
ná caithfidh mé le dlí,
's go raghad anonn thar toinn
ag comhrá leis an rí,
's mara gcuirfidh ionam aon tsuim
go dtiocfad ar ais arís
go bodach na fola duibhe
a bhain díom féin mo mhaoin.

xxxi.

Mo ghrá thú is mo mhúirnín!
Dá dtéadh mo ghlao chun cinn
go Doire Fhíonáin mór laistiar
is go Ceaplaing na n-úll buí,

How well, they could see
what a hearty bed-mate you'd be,
what a man to share a saddle with,
what a man to spark a child with.

xxx.
Jesus knows
I'll allow no bonnet to crown me
no silk slip to cover me,
no shoe to sole me
not a stitch of home furnishings
not even a rein for the chestnut mare, no,
I'll spend every cent on law-men instead.
I'll even go overseas
to confront royalty,
and if the king won't entertain me,
I'll turn again wildly
to the black-blooded lout
who thieved my treasure from me.

xxxi.
O my love and my sweetheart!
Should my howl reach as far
as grand Derrynane
and gold-appled Ceaplaing,

is mó marcach éadrom groí
is bean chiarsúra bháin gan teimheal
a bheadh anso gan mhoill
ag gol os cionn do chinn
a Airt Uí Laoghaire an ghrinn.

xxxii.
Cion an chroí seo agamsa
ar mhnáibh geala an mhuilinn
i dtaobh a fheabhas a níd siad sileadh
i ndiaidh mharcaigh na lárach doinne.

xxxiii.
Greadadh croí cruaidh ort
a Sheáin Mhic Uaithne!
Más breab a bhí uaitse
nár tháinig faoim thuairim,
's go dtabharfainn duit mórchuid:
capall gruagach
'dhéanfadh tú fhuadach
trí sna sluaitibh
lá do chruatain;
nó macha breá 'bhuaibh duit,
nó caoire ag breith uan duit,
nó culaith an duine uasail
idir spor agus buatais –

strong, the slim horsemen
and pale-hankied women
who would thunder in,
and their wails would be boundless
over Art, our own sweet scoundrel.

xxxii.
All my heart's fondness
to the bright little mill-women,
so skilled was their weeping
for the chestnut mare's horseman.

xxxiii.
Your heart, I wish broken,
John Cooney, you villain!
If it was a bribe you were seeking,
you should have come straight to me,
for I'd have given you plenty:
a horse of thick-mane
to dash you away
from the wild mobs
who await your judgment day;
pastures of cattle
or plump ewes in lamb,
or perhaps even the suit of my own gallant man,
with his own bright spurs and his fine boots too,

cé gur mhór an trua liom
í fheiscint thuas ort,
mar cloisim á luachaint
gur boidichín fuail tú.

xxxiv.

A mharcaigh na mbán-ghlac,
ó leagadh do lámh leat,
éirigh go dtí Baldwin,
an spreallairín gránna,
an fear caol-spágach,
is bain de sásamh
in ionad do lárach
is úsáid do ghrá ghil.
Gan an seisear mar bhláth air!
Gan dochar do Mháire,
agus ní le grá dhi,
ach is í mo mháthair
thug leaba 'na lár di
ar feadh trí ráithe.

xxxv.

Mó ghrá thú agus mo rún!
Tá do stácaí ar a mbonn,
tá do bha buí á gcrú;

although it'd be a wrench
to see you wear them instead,
since you're a right pissy bodkin,
or so I've heard said.

xxxiv.
O my white-grasped horseman,
Since your hand's been struck down,
why not rise up to Baldwin now,
that shit-talking clown,
that bockety wimp, all mean frowns,
to demand satisfaction
for the loss of your mare
and your beloved's heartache.
May none of his six children blossom for him!
Only let no harm fall on Mary,
and not for much sisterly love,
but only that my own mother
made her a first bed within her,
where we shared three seasons together.

xxxv.
O, my love and my darling!
Your barley has risen thick and golden,
your fair cows are well-milked,

is ar mo chroí atá do chumha
ná leigheasfadh Cúige Mumhan
ná Gaibhne Oileáin na bhFionn.
Go dtiocfaidh Art Ó Laoghaire chugham
ní scaipfidh ar mo chumha
atá i lár mo chroí á bhrú,
dúnta suas go dlúth
mar a bheadh glas a bheadh ar thrúnc
's go raghadh an eochair amú.

xxxvi.
A mhná so amach ag gol
stadaidh ar bhur gcois
go nglaofaidh Art Mhac Conchubhair deoch,
agus tuilleadh thar cheann na mbocht,
sula dtéann isteach don scoil –
ní ag foghlaim léinn ná port,
ach ag iompar cré agus cloch.

but such pain grips my heart still
that all of Munster cannot fix me a remedy,
nor even Fair Island's gifted smithery.
Unless Art Ó Laoghaire returns to me
this grief will never be eased,
it weighs on my heart so brutally,
keeping it sealed so tightly
as a lock clasps a chest
whose golden key has been lost from me.

xxxvi.
Oh, you women who cry outside,
halt your feet a while,
let Conor's son Art call a drink
and more for the other poor souls,
for soon, they'll all enter that school together –
in pursuit of neither learnèd song nor verse,
but only to raise cold stone and earth.

acknowledgements

I am grateful to the Lannan Foundation for their extraordinary generosity, which sustained me throughout the completion of this work, and to the Arts Council of Ireland, whose award of a bursary in literature at a crucial early moment allowed me the time to dream this book from seed to seedling. In the years in which I was writing these pages, I was kindly supported by Lorraine Maye and Cork Midsummer Festival, and by the wonderful women who watched my children while I tiptoed away to write: Rose, Michelle, and Marian. My gratitude also to Clíodhna Shaffrey and Michael Hill at Temple Bar Gallery, to Words Ireland, to Clare Arts Office, and to Joanna Walsh for generous encouragement. I have long admired the work of Lisa Coen, Sarah Davis-Goff, and Laura Waddell at Tramp Press, and it was my dream that they would publish this book – thank you. Mo bhuíochas leo siúd a spreag misneach ionam – to those who encouraged me to keep writing about Eibhlín Dubh, particularly when I doubted myself: Cal Doyle, Clara Dupuis-Morency, Anakana Schofield, Patricia Coughlan, Clair Wills, Linda Connolly, and Sarah-Maria Griffin. Mo bhuíochas freisin le Eoin Seartal, John Fitzgerald, Seán Ua Súilleabháin, Seán Cronin, Timmy O'Connor, Tadhg O'Sullivan, Dr Aoife Bhreatnach, agus Maureen Kennelly as ucht a gcuid nodanna. I am indebted to Brendan Barrington at *The Dublin Review*, who published early versions of two chapters and in doing so offered me exceptional editorial guidance. To Dr Dermot Mahony, in admiration. To Dr Michael Crotty, in gratitude. To Dr Suzanne O'Sullivan, a hero. To all who work for human milk banks and in NICUs. To Paula Meehan, connoisseuse of bees. To the generous librarians of Cork City, who hefted many, many armfuls of books on my behalf. To Sara Baume, whose friendship heartens me every day. To Amy and to Saoirse, who cared for me when I was afraid. To Sinéad Gleeson, for her kindness. To Matthew Turner, for guidance. To my parents: it cannot be easy to bear the embarrassment of a writer in the family, and yet you understand that I must write my own life, a gift for which I will forever be grateful. To my Nana Mae, a woman of great heart and great courage, from whom I have learned so much. All my love to my children, as always, and to Tim, for the snip. Míle buíochas ó chroí libh go léir.

further reading

As basis for my translation I attended closely to the version published by Seán Ó Tuama in his 1961 publication *Caoineadh Airt Uí Laoghaire*, and I am grateful for his impeccable scholarship. Many additional books, translations, and scholarly works have detailed the era and literature explored in this book. The following publications were of particular interest to me in constructing my own understanding of this subject, and may also be of interest to readers who wish to learn more.

Mrs Morgan John O'Connell (1892) *The Last Colonel of the Irish Brigade: Count O'Connell and Old Irish Life at Home and Abroad, 1745–1833*

Méadhbh Nic an Airchinnigh (2012) 'Caointeoireacht na Gaeilge: Béalaireacht agus Literathacht', PhD thesis, NUIG

Eugene O'Connell (2009) 'The House of Art O'Leary', *Cork Literary Review* Volume 13

Peter O'Leary (1998) 'The Life and Times of Art Ó Laoghaire', a talk given on 13 September 1998 to the third O'Leary gathering in Inchigeelagh and subsequently published in the *Journal of the Ballingeary & Inchigeela Historical Society*

Eavan Boland (2011) *A Journey with Two Maps*

Peter Levi (1984) *The Lamentation of the Dead*

Seán Ó Tuama (1995) *Repossessions*

Angela Bourke (2017) '"A Bhean Úd Thall!" Macallaí Idirghaelacha i bhFilíocht Bhéil na mBan', *Scottish Studies* Volume 37

Angela Bourke (1993) 'More in Anger than in Sorrow: Irish Women's Lament Poetry' in *Feminist Messages: Coding in Women's Folk Culture*

Angela Bourke (2002) *The Field Day Anthology of Irish Writing*, Volume IV, pp 1372–84

Edward MacLysaght (1944) 'Survey of Documents in Private Keeping: First Series – Conner Papers' *Analecta Hibernica* Volume 15, pp 153, 155–159

James O'Leary (1993) 'A Dead Man in Carriganorthane' in *A Time that Was in Clondrohid, Macroom, Millstreet, Kilnamartyra and Ballyvourney*

John T. Collins, 'Arthur O'Leary, the Outlaw' and subsequent supplements in *Journal of the Cork Historical and Archaeological Society*, Volume 54 (1949), Volume 55 (1950) and Volume 61 (1956)